“And a work of beauty stands firm as a work of beauty,
no matter which way the wind is blowing.”

Gerry Dryansky

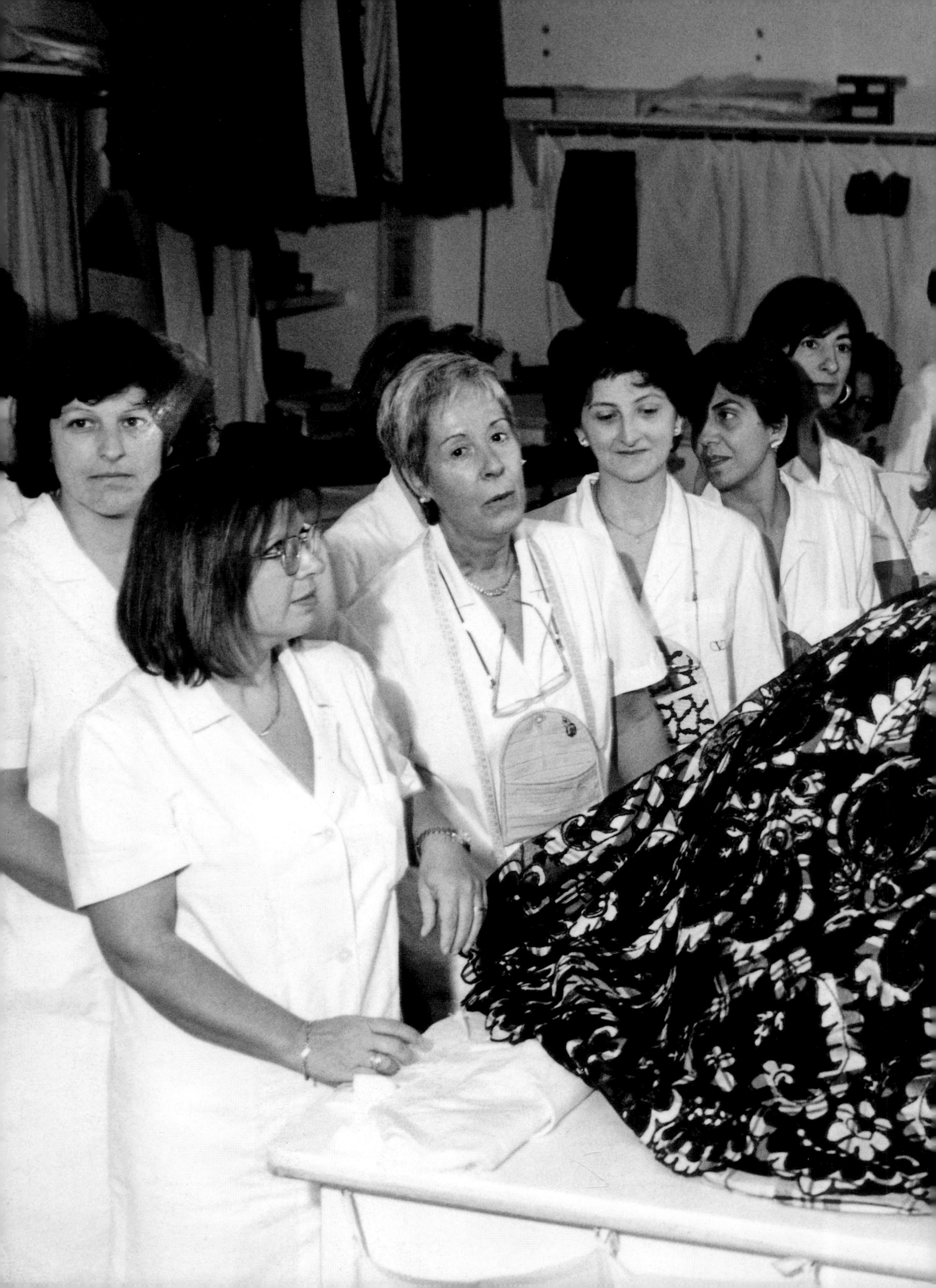

VALENTINO's magic

by
Marie Paule Pellé
text by
Patrick Mauriès

With contributions by
François Baudot
Gerry Dryansky
Bonizza Giordani Aragno
Michael Gross

Art Director
Angelo Bucarelli

ABBEVILLE PRESS PUBLISHERS
New York London Paris

Couture. Fall–Winter 1990–91.
Top covered with embroidery inspired by the late Italian Renaissance.
Photo Alfa Castaldi/Courtesy *Vogue* © 1990 Edizioni Condé Nast S.p.A.

ACKNOWLEDGMENTS

The publisher wishes to thank Valentino Garavani and Giancarlo Giammetti who consented the production of this book.

Special thanks to the photographers: Marella Agnelli, Mark Arbeit, David Bailey, Alexandre Bailhache, Dick Ballarian, Mauro Balletti, Serge Barbeau, Giampaolo Barbieri, Cecil Beaton, Jonathan Becker, Leombruno Bodi, Sergio Caminata, Alfa Castaldi, Alex Chatelain, Patrick Chevalier, Walter Chin, Jouanny Christophe, Henry Clarke, Michel Comte, Attilio Concari, Bela Cseh, Gary Deane, Alberto Dell'Orto, Patrick Demarchelier, Bernard Descamps, Terence Donovan, Sante D'Orazio, Arthur Elgort, Fabrizio Ferri, Robert Frankenberg, Robert Freson, Angelo Frontoni, Giovanni Gastel, Isidoro Genovese, Cristina Ghergo, Gianni Giansanti, Oberto Gili, Marco Glaviano, Jean-Paul Goudeaut, Janos Grapow, Renato Grignaschi, Elsa Haerter, François Halard, Hiro, Marc Hispard, Dominique Issermann, J. Noël L'Harmeroult, Peter Hönnemann, Horst P. Horst, Frank Horvat, Daniel Jouanneau, Art Kane, Neil Kirk, Eddy Kohli, Bob Krieger, Susan Lamér, François Lamy, Marco Lanza, Barry Lategan, David Lees, François Leroy Beaulieu, Peter Lindbergh, Stan Malinowsky, Stefano Massimo, Eamonn J. McCabe, Barry McKinley, Steven Meisel, Avi Meroz, Sheila Metzner, Sarah Moon, Walter Mori, Christian Moser, Ugo Mulas, Nadir, Helmut Newton, Carlo Orsi, Norman Parkinson, Irving Penn, Denis Piel, Daniel Povda, Rico Puhlmann, Karen Radkaï, Vittoriano Rastelli, Jim Reiher, Regi Relang, Willy Rizzo, Matthew Rolston, Paolo Roversi, Herbert Rowan, Galen Rowell, Franco Rubartelli, Satoshi Saikusa, Francesco Scavullo, Lothar Schmidt, David Seidner, Bill Silano, Lord Snowdon, Bob Stern, Peter Strube, John Swannell, K. Taira, Mario Testino, Toni Thorimbert, Alberta Tiburzi, Oliviero Toscani, Deborah Turbeville, Tyen, Fritz von der Schulenburg, Pietro Vaccari, Max Vadukul, Javier Vallhonrat, Luigi Volpe, Ellen von Unwerth, Chris von Wangenheim, Albert Watson, Alexandre Weinberger, Claus Wickrath, Susan Wood, Yokosuka.

Sincere thanks to the illustrators: Mats Gustavson, Michael Meyring.

Thanks also to the models: Amalia, Amira, Daniela Azzone, Paloma Bailey, Benedetta Barzini, Stefania Belletti, Marisa Berenson, Bonnie Berman, Brinja, Josie Borain, Cecilia Chancellor, Helena Christensen, Pat Cleveland, Dalma, Diane de Witt, Aly Dunne, Vanessa Duve, Gail Elliot, Linda Evangelista, Lisa Garber, Jasmine Ghauri, Daniela Ghione, Simonetta Gianfelice, Giselle, Jill Goodacre, Jerry Hall, Patty Hanson, Anjelica Huston, Lauren Hutton, Iman, Elaine Irwin, Jasmine, Sarah Kapp, Laura Killer, Kirat, Elena Kodoura, Lynne Koester, Betty Lago, Yasmin Le Bon, Dona Luna, Magali, Marpessa, Maddalena Mosca, Elsa Peretti, Mirella Petteni, Paulina Porizkova, Lisa Ruttledge, Marina Schiano, Claudia Schiffer, Sonia Schnetzer, Danka Schröder, Khoudia Seye, Tara Shannon, Brooke Shields, Diamante Spencer, Isa Stoppi, Alberta Tiburzi, Christy Turlington, Rosanne Vela, Veruschka, Eva Vorris, Leslie Winner.

Further thanks to: Peter Arnold Inc., *Amica*, Camera Press, The Condé Nast Publications Inc., Condé Nast Verlag GmbH, *Donna*, Edizioni Condé Nast S.p.A., *Elle, Frankfurter Allgemeine Magazin, Harper's Bazaar Italia, Harpers' & Queen Magazine, House & Garden, Joyce*, Les Publications Condé Nast S.A., *Madame, Moda, Moda In*, Mondadori Press, Grazia Neri, *Paris Match, L'Officiel*, Sotheby's, Studio Filomeno, Sygma, Verlag Hans Schöner, Visual Team, *WWD*.

In the Maison Valentino the help of Daniela Giardina, Carlos Souza, Loredana Di Fusco, Grazia Martino and Violante Valdettaro was invaluable. Thanks also to Adriano Castroni for his graphic support.

First published in the United States of America in 1998
by Abbeville Press, 22 Cortlandt Street, New York, NY 10007
First published in Italy in 1998
by Leonardo Arte srl, Via Trentacoste 7, 20134 Milan

Translation
Lucia Borro
Ann Goldstein
Carol Lee Rathman

The text of this book was set in New Baskerville.
Printed and bound in Italy.

First edition
2 4 6 8 10 9 7 5 3 1

Library of Congress has cataloged the previous edition as follows:
Pellé, Marie Paule.
Valentino: thirty years of magic / by Marie Paule Pellé;
texts by Patrick Mauriès; with contributions by François Baudot /... [et al.]
- 1st ed. p. cm. ISBN 1-55859-237-7
1. Valentino. 2. Costume design—Italy. 3. Costume designers-Italy—
Biography. I. Mauriès, Patrick, 1952. II. Title. TT507.P37 1990
746.9'.2'.092—dc 20 [B] 91-10337 CIP

ISBN 0-7892-0463-0

Cover
Couture. Fall–Winter 1990–91.
Close-fitting short suit in beige chiffon
embroidered with red, gold, brown, and rhinestone sequins
in an Oriental pattern.
Photo Paolo Roversi/Courtesy *Vogue* © Les Publications Condé Nast S.A.

Back Cover
Boutique. Spring–Summer 1990.
Long crêpe dress with black and white vertical stripes.
Photo Jacques Olivar.

Endpapers
Cannes. 1996.
Sharon Stone with Valentino at the Film Festival.
Photo Courtesy *Paris Match.*

Pages 4-5
Rome. 1995.
Claudia Schiffer in Valentino's atelier.
Photo Arthur Elgort/Archivio Valentino.

Page 6
Bare-backed black velvet dress with black satin bow.
Photo Dominique Issermann/Courtesy *Vogue.*
© Les Publications Condé Nast S.A.

Page 11
Couture. Fall–Winter 1965–66.
Photo Pietro Vaccari/Archivio Valentino.

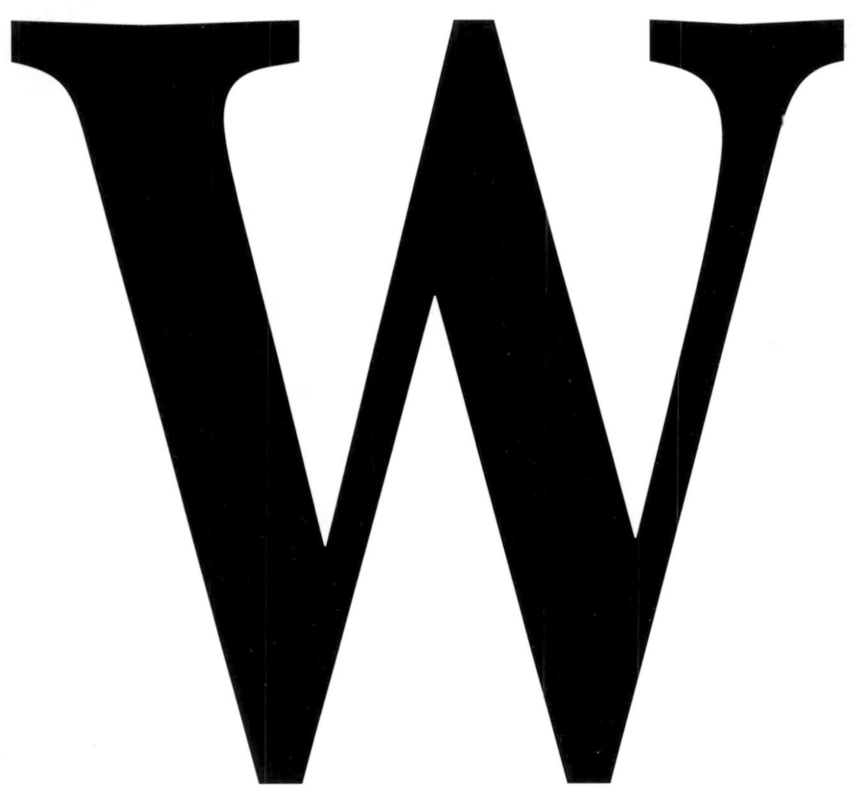

omen wearing Valentino do not toil in factories. They do not consider themselves commonplace. They do consider themselves in Cap d'Antibes, Clardige's, and Le Cirque.

Women wearing Valentino can be found lounging poolside in Capri. Skiing in Gstaad. Running board meetings in Manhattan. They can be anywhere, but they aren't everywhere. Valentino's women make a dinner meaningful and magnificent; they do not make dinner. I see them strutting down a long Paris runway—Jackie O., Jayne Wrightsman, Babe Paley, Gloria Guinness, Marella Agnelli—and striding forward in a line radiating power tempered by grace. Probably they are striding toward lunch in the garden at the Ritz, or in some *hôtel particulier* on the rue de Grenelle.

Look at them. You can't help it. Their necks are all long and erect, their shoulders straight, their stance kinetic, their legs lean and ready—always a step ahead.

Women wearing Valentino. They may like lace and fantasy but these are no Little Bo Peeps. Neither are they thoroughbreds, whippets or gazelles, though they have the legs for it. They are not cute. They are not coy. They are neither the victims nor the perpetrators of crimes of fashion.

They are not about Desire either. Rather, they are about certain highly cultivated desires. They are romantic. They are not easy.

Women wearing Valentino. For there are no such things as Valentino girls. There is nothing unformed about them. Not even Brooke Shields, who was still like a virgin when she appeared in a Valentino on the cover of *Time* magazine illustrating "The Eighties Look." Some virgin. Even though Valentino's work harkens back to times past, it is rooted, strong as an ancient tree, in the contemporary idea and exercise of womanly power.

Even in dark glasses the eyes of Valentino's woman flash with knowledge. Even in a little nothing black dress, she is something. Really something.

"A woman must cause heads to turn when she enters a room," Valentino has said. "A woman does not want to disappear."

Valentino's woman sets heads spinning.

That's because women wearing Valentino have power that crosses national, political, professional, and social lines. His clique encompasses the wives and mistresses of

Milanese industrialists, Roman countesses, and an Iranian empress, Italian and American first ladies, Niarchoses, Agnellis, Rothschilds, Fords, Lollobrigida, and Veruschka. And when these women cross lines of their own, quite often they wear Valentino.

Take Jacqueline Bouvier Kennedy on the day she married Aristotile Onassis. She was telling the world—and herself—something that day. And she chose a Valentino—a beige lace top and flyaway skirt. Couture, of course. Goodbye first lady. Hello Jackie O. What a knockout.

Women wearing Valentino are all different. Their line veers like a signature V from right bank to left bank, east coast to west, Farah Diba to Farrah Fawcett.

And yet, women wearing Valentino have more than a logo in common. Valentino women don't borrow their personality from clothes. Audrey Hepburn doesn't get her grace from a gown. Liz Taylor is never lost in her jewels and embroidery. Power like that wielded by Nancy Reagan or Georgette Mosbacher cannot be merely a matter of pale flesh and paper taffeta. Like them or not, these "ladies" are contenders.

Glamorous and elegant, softly tailored and a little conservative, but not unaware of the lures and liefs of decadence, Valentino's women populate all the best places, knowing that they have what it takes to pass unmolested through even the worst of times.

Not that they see many bad times. Women wearing Valentino are simply a cut above.

Michael Gross

Page 12
Rome, 1972.
Valentino with his public
at the close of a show.
Photo Courtesy *Vogue* © 1972
Edizioni Condé Nast S.p.a.

Page 15
Couture. Spring–Summer 1963.
Drawing Michael Meyring.

VOGUE
Paris

VALENTINO
Spring '63

Jacket,
zebra printed
calfskin—
jet-embroidered
passementerie

Skirt,
white silk

Worn by
Simone d'Aillencourt

Rome. Atelier Couture 1990.
Valentino fashioning a dress on one of his models.
Photo Lord Snowdon/Camera Press/Grazia Neri.

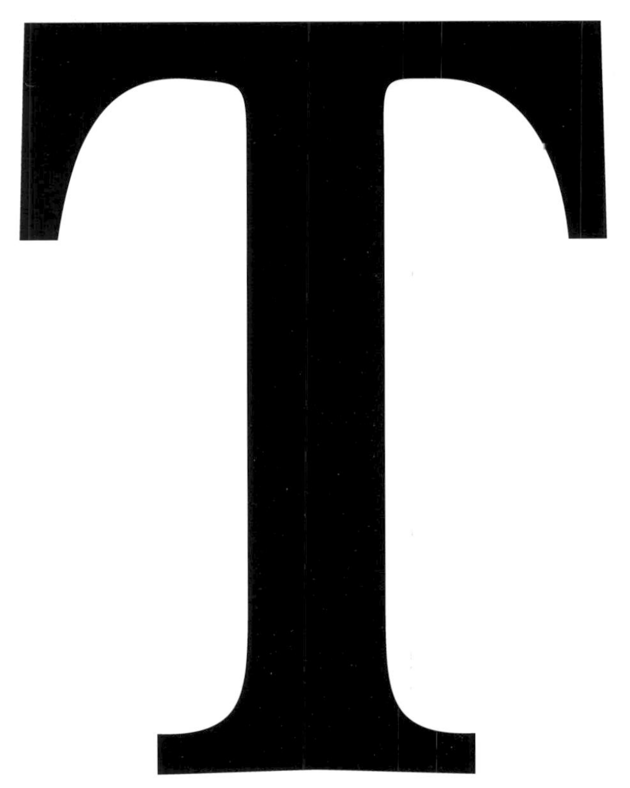

he myth of the artist exists: forty years ago two Central European intellectuals conducted a scholarly study and wrote the definitive results in a few pages. The myth of the *couturier* also exists; but it has yet to be written, being a mere corollary of the former.

Valentino cannot be overlooked in this respect; indeed, he offers a shining example of it. As a child he paid no attention to activities supposedly suited "to his age"; he was not the least bit interested in fun and games, the small rivalries, the great inseparable friendships, the scoldings, and the ballgames; he was already obsessed with the paper sewing patterns that his aunt's notions business was so rich in; he was trying, and with some success, to sketch out figures and styles—auspicious foreshadowings of a pure dreamworld made up of quintessential forms, lightness, luxury.

This all happened in Voghera, a small town of Lombardy that would later claim Valentino, as they would have said in classical times, as its ornament. No foreigner can estimate what an Italian's "homeland" represents to him, adopted or by right of birth, roots that he fiercely defends and that define his very being once and for all. I once overheard a young girl in a restaurant shrug off a flaw in her companion's personality as due to his Brescian heritage. Every city, town, region, and neighborhood has its own creative principles that determine physiognomy and substance, culinary and aesthetic tastes, accents and erotic nuances—and especially world outlooks certainly.

But this is the point: Valentino is one of those rare, aberrant Italians for whom geographical sentiments seem to have next to no importance. In Voghera he was born in 1932; there he lived out an apparently happy adolescence; and from Voghera he departed in 1950 to follow the path of his desire or his obsessions, not to return until many years later on the occasion of his deification, the above-mentioned recognition (you may forget your origins, but they never forget you).

Let us return to our discussion of the myth of the *couturier*. Ever since he can remember he dreamed of but one thing, one world; some years later (we are skipping way ahead) he found himself at the center of this world, as real as he had desired. This lightning course, this extraordinary blossoming, was ensured by just a few intermediaries, a handful of wild cards: a mother, Paris, one or more muses, a friend and partner.

Let us now trace the succession of events that helped to create the legend: episodes endlessly repeated, similar to what everybody has experienced in the immediate family circle, anecdotes rehashed over and over at ritual get-togethers until one cannot take it any more; or blown up with evident relish beyond all recognition by the press when it is a matter of "out of the ordinary" figures. Nevertheless, these scenes and fragments of stories manage to conserve, even after all the repetition, their exemplary and revelatory value.

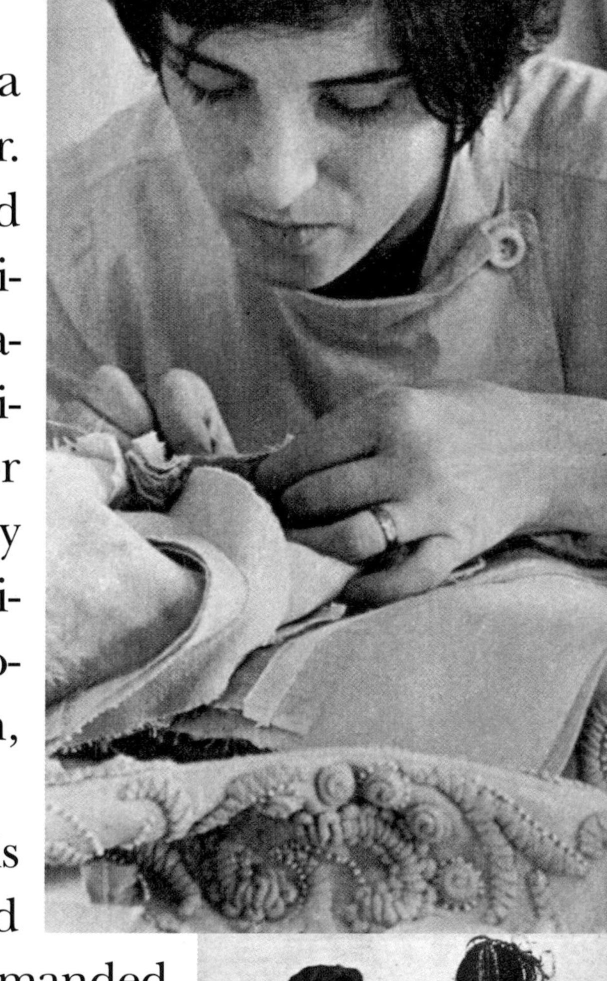

So, there is a child who has eyes only for the materials and the textures that surround us, the shapes behind which we hide ourselves, and which we need. He demanded from his parents made-to-measure clothing in the finest wools and cashmeres, with *that* collar and *that* cut; he could not bear slovenliness, or lack of respect for one's person. At a young age, he chose only to see and to take interest in the "beautiful and the good", as the ancient Greeks would say; he could conceice only of a reality mastered, distilled, subjected to the law of aesthetics. Once he had to make an appearance at a little party given in honor of his cousin, though he was ill. He asked someone to help him over to admire his cousin's party attire, and the emotion aroused in him by the rustling fabric was so strong that to this day he remembers the rose-colored tulle dress that the fortunate young girl wore on that day; as he was to remember his wonder at the rustling of a black crêpe de chine skirt with green polka dots made for his mother by the Costa sisters, renowned *couturières* of Voghera; or the softness of a coat in *grain de poudre* trimmed with a fox-fur collar.

1. Rome. Laboratory: handcrafted workmanship of an Haute-Couture dress. Photo Robert Freson/Archivio Valentino.
2. Couture. Spring–Summer 1959. Valentino presents a print dress with crinoline skirt. Photo Archivio Valentino.
3. Rome, 1959. Valentino in his atelier at the work table. Photo Lord Snowdon/Archivio Valentino.

Nothing but passions, delectable passions; or, if you like, the signs of destiny. May it suffice to desire, said Nietzsche, to achieve one's happiness. And while Valentino's trajectory to success bears out this formula, it also goes to show that he always knew what he wanted, and that he unerringly followed the road that opened out before him, taking advantage of all the imponderables, the strokes of luck, predestinations, and complex legacies.

"An almost infantile belief," he says himself, "in the possibility of getting out of life what I want." To believe that all is allowed or possible has been the guiding light in his life, alongside a strange form of self-knowledge. In our everyday culture we are surrounded by references to astrology, and the fact of belonging to one of the signs (in this case, Taurus) is not always met with indifference; when it is not seen as an archaic holdover of superstitious beliefs, it seems to charge the person in question with an inrush of energies.

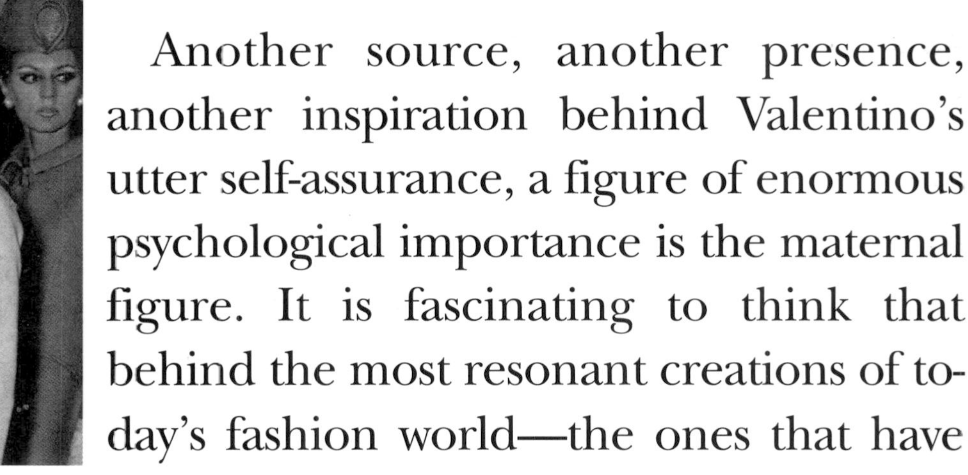

Another source, another presence, another inspiration behind Valentino's utter self-assurance, a figure of enormous psychological importance is the maternal figure. It is fascinating to think that behind the most resonant creations of today's fashion world—the ones that have enjoyed the greatest popular success—behind the revolution in our everyday appearance, stand a handful of elegant provincial ladies of mid-century, who were more decisive in the vicissitudes of fashion than the great buyers or other legendary figures in the history of elegance.

Look at hos Saint Laurent, Lacroix, and Valentino evoke, a mother's leaving for the ball, a trail of perfume, a hat (when it was still *de rigueur*) with its halo of chiffon, a necklace, a cock-

1. 1959. Valentino at a New York reception. Photo Archivio Valentino.
2. Couture. Spring–Summer 1967. Valentino and his models.
Presentation of the collection at the Martha Award ceremony in New York.
3. Couture. Fall–Winter 1959–60.
Ball gown with ivory-colored satin cape. Photo Archivio Valentino.

Page 20
Rome, 1991. Valentino at the Campidoglio.
Photo Gianni Giansanti/ArchivioValentino.

tail dress carefully chosen for a meeting with her lady friends. These traces leave burning impressions on one's childhood and long after their disappearance leave a mark, like a retinal after-image upon our memory. Although fashion is seemingly the art most rooted in the present, it is in fact paradoxically supported by distant reminiscences imbued with happy nostalgia; it is the inevitable form of homage that a period pays to its yesterday.

Not that these involve solemn commemorations, nor do they refer to great moments or the most important events of a given period; rather they focus on a multitude of accents that make up the ordinary, and whose destiny is to disappear with their day. Traces of them remain in that slight moment of hesitation, suspended for just one last instant in such details as the design of a pocket, the cut of a sandal, the color of a taffeta, the pattern of a print. At the age of fifteen, the young Valentino Garavani realized once and for all that it would be a mistake to continue in the field of geometrical sketches and drawings; his real interest lay in the freehand variations of fashion design. He calmly and frankly opened

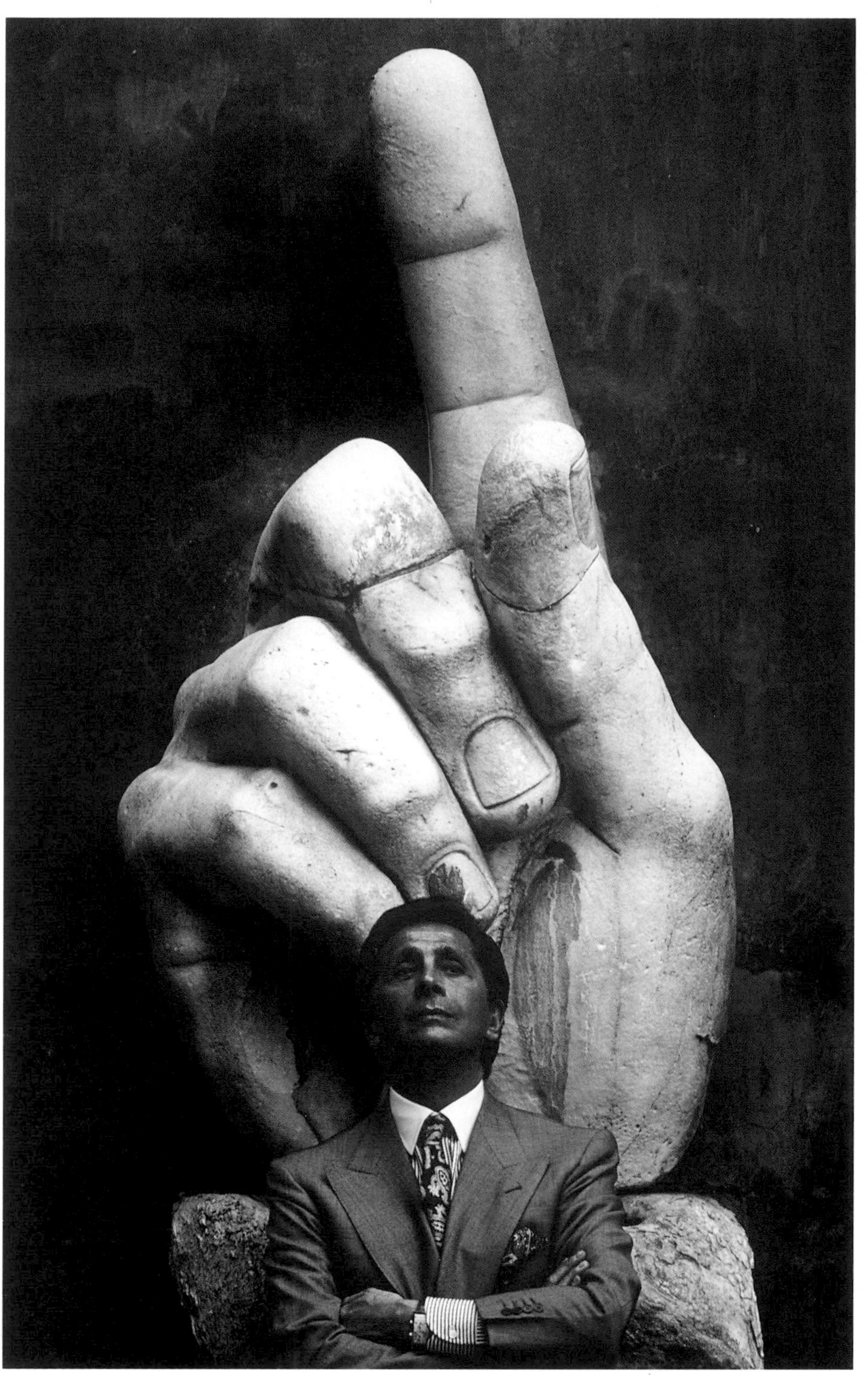

his heart to his parents and stated his intention to quit high school without taking his final examinations in order to take the plunge into the world of high fashion. There was the predictable moment of shock and alarm, which could only give way to resignation, given the young man's no less predictable determination. So, armed with his parents' blessing and his innately methodical approach to things, he spent a few months in Milan to study French and to take courses in fashion design at a school in via Santa Marta. It was a period of apprenticeship, a period of transition before setting his foot inside that magic ring—the place for which Valentino will never cease to feel an unremitting sense of awe: Paris, capital of clothing and of *savoir-faire*, of hostesses and balls, of the spirit of a time.

Valentino arrived in Paris in 1950. Three years earlier, a name had become a household word : overnight Dior took his place at the helm of fashion, launching a style that was to represent an epoch. It was a return to petticoat, to the eighteenth century revisited by Napoléon III, to Louis XVI style; it was the time when Arturo Lopez recreated a miniature Versailles in downtown Neuilly, Charles de Beistegui took possession of the Palazzo Labia in Venice, and Emilio Terry set his imagination to work on the "Louis XVII" style.

No less than twenty-five or twenty-six yards of taffeta were needed to obtain the volume of such suggestively named lines as *Corolle*, *Cyclone*, *Tulipe*, *Oblique*, *Sinueuse*, *Verticale*, not to mention the fifty yards of black plait that edged the neck and hemlines of a 1947 model. Shameless expenditures, exaggerated shapes, and voluminous materials became all the rage in a society that had just emerged from the privations of the war. The contrast was striking: the daily economy was laboriously recovering while inordinate fortunes were being spectacularly squandered in a wild contest to achieve absolute luxury. It was getting difficult, reported a society journal of the time, to keep track of "*les nuits de*" this and the "*les quinzaines de*" that. The two hundred fiftieth anniversary of the Place Vendôme was celebrated, the fiftieth of the Métro, the one hundred fiftieth of the Conseil d'Etat. Ladies arrived at the balls on camelback or carried in litters, dressed up as firebirds, Cleopatras, angels of Versailles, Lancret's Harlequins. This was also the golden age of the sculptural and slender muses: Mitza Bricard and runway model Renée for Dior, Liza Fonsagrives for Irving Penn, Dovima for Avedon, Patricia Lopez Willshaw, Maxime de la Falaise, Audrey Hepburn; all creatures with long, swanlike

Spring–Summer 1959.
Drawing by Valentino: Ibis line.

necks underlined with pearls, accentuated by décolleté, with slim waists and hips emphasized by peplums; gloved, hatted, *soignées*, as the designer's pet word so aptly describes them.

Armed with a grant from the Chambre Syndicale de la Haute Couture Parisienne, Valentino landed in Jean Dessès's atelier where he stayed for five years, "like at university," before moving on to spend two years with Guy Laroche (of Dessès little else remains today but a perfume in a fine white felt-lined box, evocatively named "Bal à Versailles," the last trace of the sumptuous mid-twentieth-century dream). But the sparkle of this period seems to stem from a burning fascination with the art of living. He was discovering this in the salon of Jacqueline de Ribes, a graphic creature with high cheekbones, almond-shaped eyes, a remarkably fine nose, and tapered hands more suited to caressing things than to taking hold of them.

Unconsciously, she offered herself to a gaze dazzled by so much natural "civility." Valentino was fascinated by her three or four changes of *toilette* per day, by her way of serving tea, moving, selecting her attire, seating her guests, decorating a table, by her tone of voice, her love of accessories, the confidence of her gestures, a way of crossing her legs, a trail of perfume.

"*La donna immaginaria*," said a baroque Italian aesthete of the seventeenth century. The woman who does not exist, who has never been nor shall be, said Saint-Evremond; such is the dazzling specter that took root in Valentino's imagination and the styles he produced—in the form of so many flashes, flickers of memory, blazes of inspiration. This ideal woman oriented all of his later production, his concept of dress, without restricting him to a historical frame of reference or dating him. It was an essence that was embodied in the rustling of taffeta; in the contour of a neckline; in a fabric that was never quite silky, abundant, rich, or sculptural enough for him; and in a boundless sensual pleasure in spending and in the imponderable.

After seven years of apprenticeship of unusual happiness, Valentino returned to Italy to open an atelier on via Condotti in Rome, near such stars—by then fading from the scene—as Schubert and the Fontana sisters. Boutiques that preserved a bit of the discretion, the intimate side of the family *couturier*, while still belonging by full rights to the exigent and extravagant world of the Haute Couture. This was also the peak season of such greats as Lancetti, Fabiani, Antonelli, Emilio Pucci, and a singular and rigorous architect named Roberto Capucci. The legendary designer took his first faltering steps; his parents offered him several million lire with which he financed his first *maison de couture*. And at this time Valentino was dealt the final winning card in his game, his alter ego: the man who filled, as the need arose, the posts of administrator and financier, a behind-the-scenes figure who made the dream possible.

July 30, 1960: sitting at an outdoor café on one of those seductively sweet Roman evenings, a young student of architecture watches the approach of a lively group led by a young man, a rising star of the Italian fashion scene who had already attracted notice for some remarkable accomplishments. Though we have no eyewitness reports, we are perfectly familiar with the scene, the toy shop and *parrucchiere* Millefiori to one side and the tobacconist on the other. The Café de Paris, bordered with flower pots, is saturated by a piercing light that dances in a glittering display over the chrome trim of cars, the lenses of dark glasses, coffee cups, and novelty brooches that the bescarved *mondaines* of the time were so fond of.

On via Veneto, then, of which we have a minutely detailed copy made in August of the previous year in Studio 5 of Cinecittà, as close in detail as it could be even if the original was sinuously sloping while the copy was quite flat and straight. Valentino and Giancarlo Giammetti met in the heart of a Rome that was in its full glory, in the height of its season of elegance. They crossed paths again in Capri, and when one of the young fashion designer's financiers wished to retire, causing not a few problems, the twenty-one-year-old architecture student stepped in to resolve the crisis.

Even before one piece was sold, the first Roman collection became the talk of the town, affronting the nonchalant provincialism of the capital when Valentino had, *alla grande*, enticed away one of Dior's top models to put on the runway in Rome. But the true fashion center was in Florence, the meeting ground for international buyers. After a hard-fought struggle Valentino won the right to show there, almost surreptitiously, at the end of the day when the buyers and journalists are saturated. But by word of mouth—the noble and profitable version of gossip, the true life-breath of the fashion world which hungrily gobbles up news about new names, fresh reputations, potential upstarts—the unknown designer's name reached the ears of some influential people. The first act of the golden legend of Valentino took place. He made his mark with one hundred pieces setting immediately. What has blossomed today into ten seasonal collections was just then beginning to germinate.

Nevertheless, gossip amounts to nothing without the aid of its high priestesses. And whether it was a question of luck or necessity, Valentino benefited from the kindness of an extraordinary constellation of darlings and other society ladies. Leafing through the earliest of the three hundred volumes of archives housed in piazza Mignanelli reveals his legions of diaphanous ladies of Rome. These aristocrats never stepped out of their homes if they were not dressed in Valentino's latest tailleur or evening gown. Indeed they were as good as models, slightly phantasmic as they put themselves on display: the Princesses Luciana Pignatelli, Orsetta Caracciolo Torlonia, Allegra Caracciolo di Castagneto, Peggy d'Arenberg, Ira Fürstenberg. But this dazzling array of elegance risks overshadowing other even more decisive figures, such as Consuelo Crespi, at the time the pulse of the Roman office of the American edition of *Vogue*, and one of the mainsprings of Valentino's earliest success. He was also linked with the almost flamboyant artist of elegance, Diana Vreeland. As the platonic ideal of the fashion editor, she was an unlikely candidate, with a profile like a gargoyle's or a Manchurian empress's, ever poised to swoop down on the next *coup d'éclat* or the wildest innovation ("There must be no limits to either absurdity or snobbery."). She was the reigning queen of the fashion kingdom, carefully cultivating her eccentric personality and distilling her metaphysics of the frivolous in a language rich with nuance. Always on the alert and priding herself on her intuition, Vreeland was one of the first to recognize Valentino's talent, and she gave him her support with a rare constancy. This was doubtless one of the fashion designer's main channels to success. From the very beginning he shot to inernational importance, endowed by a circle of prestigious clients, Americans as well as Europeans. "Valentino Steals Spotlight" ran a July 1965 headline in the *New York Times*, and three months later *Marie-Claire* dedicated several pages to "the crazy style of Virna Lisi" and "the new Italian *couturier* with the storybook name of Valentino" who was constantly "outdoing himself in extravagance."

Couture. Spring–Summer 1989.
Valentino with Aly Dunne in a black silk evening dress.
Rome, Palazzo Mignanelli.
Photo Barry McKinley/Archivio Valentino.

The customers, ladies who represent a strange hybrid between the fairytale world and that of commerce, a royal universe and one of spectacle, pure innate grace and the expert make-over, the "black continent" as Freud described womanhood, at once far and near, familiar and unknown. It is a curious relationship that binds the fashion designer and his customer, comparable to that which we might have with an antiques dealer or to the tie between a patron and an artist. There is no doubt that it is an economic relationship, but one that also involves trust and consent and occasional rejection, going beyond the game of giving and receiving; they become accomplices in a form of partnership or sharing. Remarkably, from the very start—and thanks to the channels we mentioned above—Valentino's clientele extended beyond the select circles of Roman society to the other side of the Atlantic. Part of Valentino's fascination owes to the supereminence of his clientele, which includes countless first ladies, actresses, and prominent personalities, and involves the whole spectrum of femininity, from the young girl to the mature woman, from the full complete form of a Sophia Loren to the budding one of a Brooke Shields. Valentino's styles also show an intriguing ability to set the pace of the times. There is the famous winter coat in hazel-colored cashmere bordered in sable that Farah Diba wrapped herself in as she left for her exile. There is the little pleated skirt and lace bodice conceived for the Onassis wedding—a now legendary event—for which Valentino received no less than thirty-eight requests for copies, not necessarily coming from families of colossal wealth, but a good part of them from Italy. The canonic list of personalities in the Valentino pantheon includes Jackie Onassis and Princess Margaret, Jane Fonda and Brooke Shields, Marella Agnelli and Joan Collins, Sophia Loren and the queen of Jordan.

Couture. Spring–Summer 1989.
Giancarlo Giammetti in his studio with Aly Dunne.
Rome, Palazzo Mignanelli.
Photo Barry McKinley/Archivio Valentino.

No doubt friendship networks and a genius for public relations contributed greatly to bringing together such a set of worldly female icons; but the phenomenon is much simpler and more natural to explain. It arises from the nature of fashion design itself as Valentino knows it, his almost childlike sensual delight in sumptuous and delicate fabrics, ornate bits of embroidery, rich, deep colors, all those elements that can exalt an ideal and truly magical femininity, which in his mind can never be too extravagant, caressing, or sophisticated. It is a form of theater that is never better interpreted than by the incredible, exaggerated, filtered, altered humanity that is conferred by celebrity.

In this respect, Valentino has never changed his course. Resuming our chronological account, a photo of Versuchka that dates from about the time when the firm was established describes this personality perfectly. It is an icon of femininity in full bloom and almost cunning, a perfect enchantress Alcina, a baroque fairy witch with a broad forehead and light-colored eyes, hieratic and sensual, made-up and bejeweled, with an incredible mane of hair, the symbol of that alluring and secret otherness whose flamboyance itself is a weapon. Rarely has a model so effectively used a kind of bestiality. Veruschka's beauty arises from abnormal proportions, too-large lips and eyes, a too-fine nose, an excess of hair, feline proportions, the nimbleness of her limbs, the slenderness of waist, a bend of the wrist, a certain stride, a way of curling back on herself. The effect is a slight inebriation, a subtle unsettling, an invisible entropy of what is human. And every square inch of this extraordinary machine exuded an extreme civility that could not help but give perfect substance to Valentino's obsession with the *soigné* ("*Soigné* is the word," he said to an English journalist, "such a pity you have no English translation.").

Valentino knows intuitively that despite the illusion that accompanies our daily lives, the human body is above all made up of bits and pieces, of mismatched elements, a problem that only a master craftsmann can solve by going deeper into the illusion, searching for a vision of the whole, for a harmony that is by nature ephemeral (a penchant that finds expression in the garment industry terms total look or *coordonnées*). And everybody who has ever worked with him will bear witness to the fashion designer's care to ensure that not a model steps out onto the runway who is not perfectly coiffed, made up, perfumed, fit out with shoes, gloves, and jewelry. Extreme vigilance and methodical construction combine to create the most natural air, the most fluid movements.

Starting in 1965, Valentino's career took on the non-stop rhythm of the different seasonal "themes" in an endless succession of "lines" and "trends." The year 1968 saw the launch of the "Collection blanche" in which for the first time the *couturier's* production bore what was to become a personal hallmark: the use of white, which appears like a leitmotiv through all of his years of activity, has resurfaced in new form in the recent Hoffmann-insipired collections with their contrasting black filigree. The following years showed uncertainty about hemlines. "The miniskirt is dead once and for all. I believe that the midi is the only chance for a return to elegance," he said in an interview of 1970. Certainly, the period was marked by dramatic contrasts and reversals of tendency. The conflict hinged on a simple choice between the fresh new design of the "mini," risqué and not for everybody, and its utter opposite, a historical reference that returned women to the long-forgotten shapes of the first decaded of the century. It was an unexpected swing full of exotic overtones.

The year 1967 marked the release of a film that heralded this sharp return to the past and the presentation of a nostalgic and romantic collection: *Bonnie and Clyde*, directed by Arthur Penn. Though many years have passed, we must not overlook the fact that it ushered in an era focusing on the curious events of the 1930s and initiating a vogue that would not pass until twenty years later—after an incredible reevaluation of the style and its subjects. At the time, the English proposed dubbing this style "Longuette," but the few attempts to make it stick with the press fell through; instead Barbara Hulaniki's Biba stores headed up the commercial success of this new fashion, offering it in a hybrid form to the general public in a wide variety of inexpensive articles and clothing. Black and gold were the colors that dominated the fashion world. In less than five months the modernism and wild prints of the miniskirt era gave way to a wave of nostalgia in classical hues tending toward dark colors and straight lines. ("There is a lot of op," wrote Irene Brin in the *Giornale d'Italia* of July 20, 1965, "in the Valentino collection [...] checkered, lozenged and striped composition in black and white used in a variety of ways on short coats or suits and white bluses.")

Again it was demonstrated that, like painting in classical times or opera in the nineteenth century, film is the most important and most influential art of this century. In 1969 Luchino Visconti's *The Damned* was released, and Valentino does not deny his fascination with the film's main character, his world, and his imagination, nor that they were a source of inspiration for several collections of the time. This aristocrat with finely chiseled features, a great narcissistic and brusque lord aware of his heritage and sure of his tastes and of his yearnings after the past, showed Valentino not so much a unique aesthetic or a vague pleasure in "decadence" or a deleterious fascination for virulent beauty, but rather the importance of lifestyle, of

Couture. Fall–Winter 1967–68.
Valentino on the runway
of his Rome atelier with three models
wearing evening gowns: the first
in a brocade print inspired by Persian
carpet motifs; the second in crêpe
with embroidered garlands
was later worn by
Jacqueline Onassis in Cambodia.
Archivio Valentino

the art of living. Because, if Visconti championed a value in his life and his work, it was certainly that of aesthetics applied to the most insignificant details of our lives, to the film set as well as to a place setting for a meal, interior decoration, and conversation. The 1969–70 and 1976–77 collections are steeped in nostalgia.

In 1972 Valentino presented an Edwardian line exploiting once again this aristocratic nostalgia in its dying burst of glory. There is a long flounced skirt in a large check pattern accompanied by a transparent *faux plis* blouse with leg-of-mutton sleeves and very high collar edged with lace ruches—a nostalgic and refined style destined to an Arcadia of conventions, a rustling reverie. In retrospect it can be seen how such a play of proportions and volumes, the way of concealing the figure behind the fullness of the fabric, the rejection of structure behind this style, that hovers somewhere between the peasant and the gypsy, is now outdated in most of Europe, England excepted, additional proof that the "English scene" is the only one today (I am talking about what one sees in the streets) where skirts that drop to below the knees are still familiar and commonplace. This indicates a typical Victorianism as well as a deluxe bohemian style, an obstinate casualness, mildly transgressive, as Virginia Woolf or Vanessa Bell practiced it: headscarf and leather sandals.

Valentino was not inclined toward the very long, the very loose-fitting, the woolen and calico fabrics typical of the country look. Nevertheless, from his synthetic "Velàzquez Gypsy Look" of 1969 to the Tyrolian accents of 1977, to certain articles from more recent collections, he has remained faithful throughout his long career to folk motifs. Depending on the occasion, he borrows from the Arabic, Slavic, Indian, and Chinese traditions.

This could represent one of the poles of a recurrent opposites in his work: that of the light, veiled, transparent fabrics versus the heavily embroidered vests, bodices, and tunics, with inlay work, beads, or encrusted with multicolored threads and rhinestones that offset the suppleness of the rest, as if the designer found a point of contact with the ancient masters.

Another "ethnic" resonance emerges when visiting the meticulously kept clothing collection housed on one floor of the Palazzo Mignanelli. Very early on, Valentino showed a predilection (particularly in evening gowns) for the quilted fabrics that one often finds in the mountain regions. He also often returns to the muted tones of the the loden fabrics that are typical of the southern Alps. In 1977 he presented the "Ludwig" collection, which demonstrates a Central European tendency so common among northern Italians—a fascination with otherness that is still very close at hand, memories of a conflict-ridden period in history characterized by relationships that arise as much out of admiration as of reaction, subjection as much as emancipation (all the ambiguity represented by a voluptuous Alida Valli in *Senso* and the character of the Contessa Serpieri in the short and compelling monologue by Boito).

But Valentino arrived at this rich and diverse Central Europe through yet another device, one that makes up another constant feature of his output. In 1973 he presented a collection whose printed fabrics (for the most part crêpe georgette) took their inspiration from Gustav Klimt and a series of sumptuous dresses whose exuberant patterns and vibrant colors may well have been in homage to Léon Bakst. Fifteen

1. Valentino in his atelier with Virna Lisi wearing a dress that made history from the Spring–Summer 1965 collection. Photo Angelo Frontoni.
2. Gustav Klimt, detail of the dining room in the Palais Stoclet. Brussels, 1905–11.
3. Couture. Fall–Winter 1989–90. Shoe with embroidered motif inspired by the Jugendstil.
4. Valentino in his atelier with styles from the Fall–Winter 1967–68 collection. Photo Walter Mori/Epoca © Mondadori Press.

Page 33
Couture. Fall–Winter 1962–63. Yellow lace dress on the film set for Fellini's *8 1/2*. Photo Archivio Valentino.

years later Hoffmann was the inspiration behind the rigorous twotoned color scheme in a line that reproposed the stylized patterns of Wiener Werkstätte's friezes and ogives. This decoration was similar to that of the halls of the Accademia that Valentino opened in 1989 next door to the Palazzo Mignanelli. The Viennese never declared—as

Adolf Loos did—that decoration was a crime; rather they sought a return to both the logic and the lexicon of traditional ornament through novel applications in cabinetry, architecture, and the design of ordinary objects. Valentino shows a similar predilection when he appliqués motifs abstracted from the work of Hoffmann or others onto an article of clothing. He enjoys treating fashion as another of the decorative arts. The dress with dots and sinuous lines that he designed in 1989 is simultaneously a citation, an homage, and a creation in its own right subject to a new order, a new logic, and thus achieving utterly new associations.

Let us return to the hushed floor of the Palazo Mignanelli, with its sound-muting wall-to-wall carpeting, mirrored walls, and metal stands where the articles of clothing are carefully conserved. Labeled, described, classified, covered, cleaned, restored, they are like a very alive memento, an arresting panorama of thirty years of activity. Giancarlo Giammetti explains with a smile how this museum was put together. Nobody even remotely suspected twenty years ago the extraordinary cultural dignity that would invest these remains of a daily effort, these fragile combinations of fabrics, whose fate would have been to disappear with their time, to end up forgotten in the back of some closet. Collected, good as new, they make it possible to get a rough idea of what might be called a stylistic analysis of Valentino or at least a culling out of certain constant features and predilections that appear throughout his work.

For example, Valentino rejected the fabrics used in the sixties, such as the stiff woolens and chenilles, because they created an abstract outline, a vague geometry of the ordinary, sculpting as well as hindering the way one moved, providing a shell or a shield. Instead, he remained faithful to cloudlike fabrics, to the fluidity and suppleness of the material: crêpe georgette, woole crêpe, muslin, silk, cashmere, velvet, soft tweeds, jerseys. Missing or infrequent—because, he says, of a lack of imagination on his part—are satin or taffeta. He saves these for only the most special uses, above all for evening wear, as he still finds their application in other spheres problematic.

Materials that sheathe and cling, that marry and follow the shape of the body and the natural gait. Effects of transparency came next, and the designer loved nothing better than the superimposition of delicate fabrics, offering glimpses of a vague motif. Then came all the variations of the next-to-nothing, the aerial sculptures of the flounces, ruches, fluting, tiny pleats that support an invisible matrix, the accent on the neckline and wrists, and other discrete details. Or the ornamental may take full possession of the body, transforming it into a sinuous flower or endowing it with subtle wings. These are the famous pieces made for Brooke Shields

Photo Gianni Giansanti/Sygma/Grazia Neri.

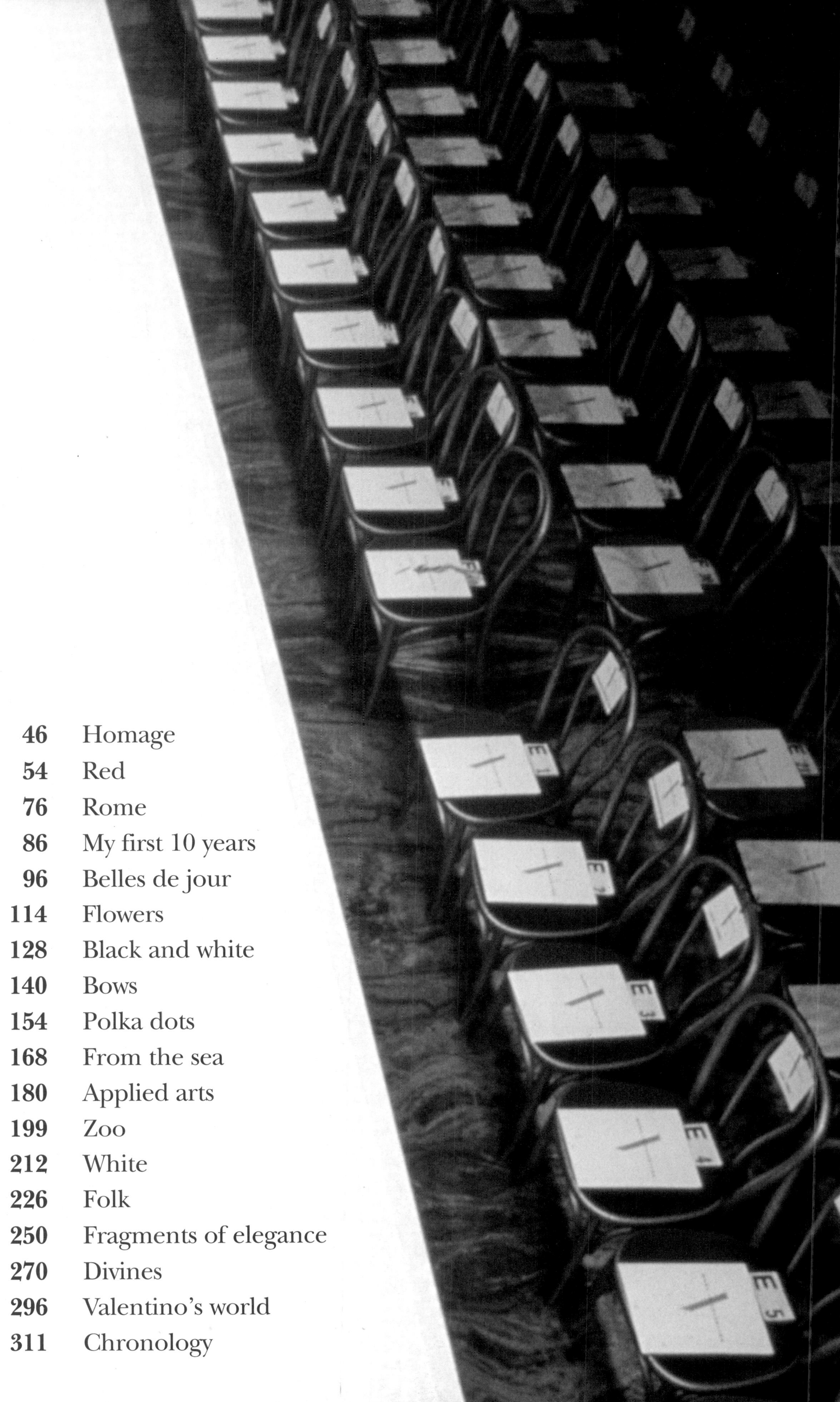

Couture. Spring–Summer 1972.
Elizabeth Taylor with Richard Burton at the Bal Proust
at Guy de Rothschild's Château Férrières.
The actress wears a black taffeta dress with vertical inserts
of Valenciennes lace and a plunging neckline with ruches
in a late nineteenth-century style.
Headpiece made of diamonds and emeralds.
Photo Cecil Beaton/Courtesy Sotheby's.

Page 48
Couture. Fall–Winter 1969–70.
Audrey Hepburn with black organdy cape.
Photo Giampaolo Barbieri.

1. Valentino and Begum Aga Khan.
2. Valentino and Joan Collins.
3. H.H. Grace of Monaco.
4. Sophia Loren.
5. Anne Getty.
6. Yasmine Khan.
7. H.R.H. Paola of Belgium.
8. Mimi Rogers and Tom Cruise.
9. Valentino and Ira Fürstenberg.
10. Luciana Pignatelli.
11. Vittoria Leone.
12. Valentino, Sharon Stone, Jeanne Moreau, Alain Delon.
13. Sofia of Hapsburg.
14. Valentino and Her Majesty the Queen Noor of Jordan.
15. Jessica Lange.
16. Isabella Rossellini.
17. Lauren Hutton.
18. Raquel Welch.
19. Diana Vreeland and Giancarlo Giammetti.
20. Pavlos and Marie Chantal of Greece.
21. Brooke Shields.
22. Giancarlo Giammetti, Maria Pia Fanfani, Gianni Agnelli.
23. Valentino and Nancy Reagan.
24. Marella Agnelli.
25. Marie Hélène de Rothschild.
26. Valentino, Giancarlo Giammetti and Lauren Bacall.
27. Domiziana Giordano.
28. Pilar Crespi.
29. Fanny Ardant.
30. H.R.H. Princess Diana of Wales and Valentino.
31. Liza Minnelli.
32. Ornella Muti.
33. Lynn Wyatt and Giancarlo Giammetti.
34. Her Majesty the Queen Sofia of Spain.
35. Dina Merrill.
36. Gloria Guinness.
Photos Archivio Valentino.

Pages 52-53
Couture. Fall–Winter 1967–68. A photograph of Jacqueline Onassis during her official visit to Cambodia. Green toga trimmed with pearl and crystal beads. Photo Archivio Valentino.

LORIA

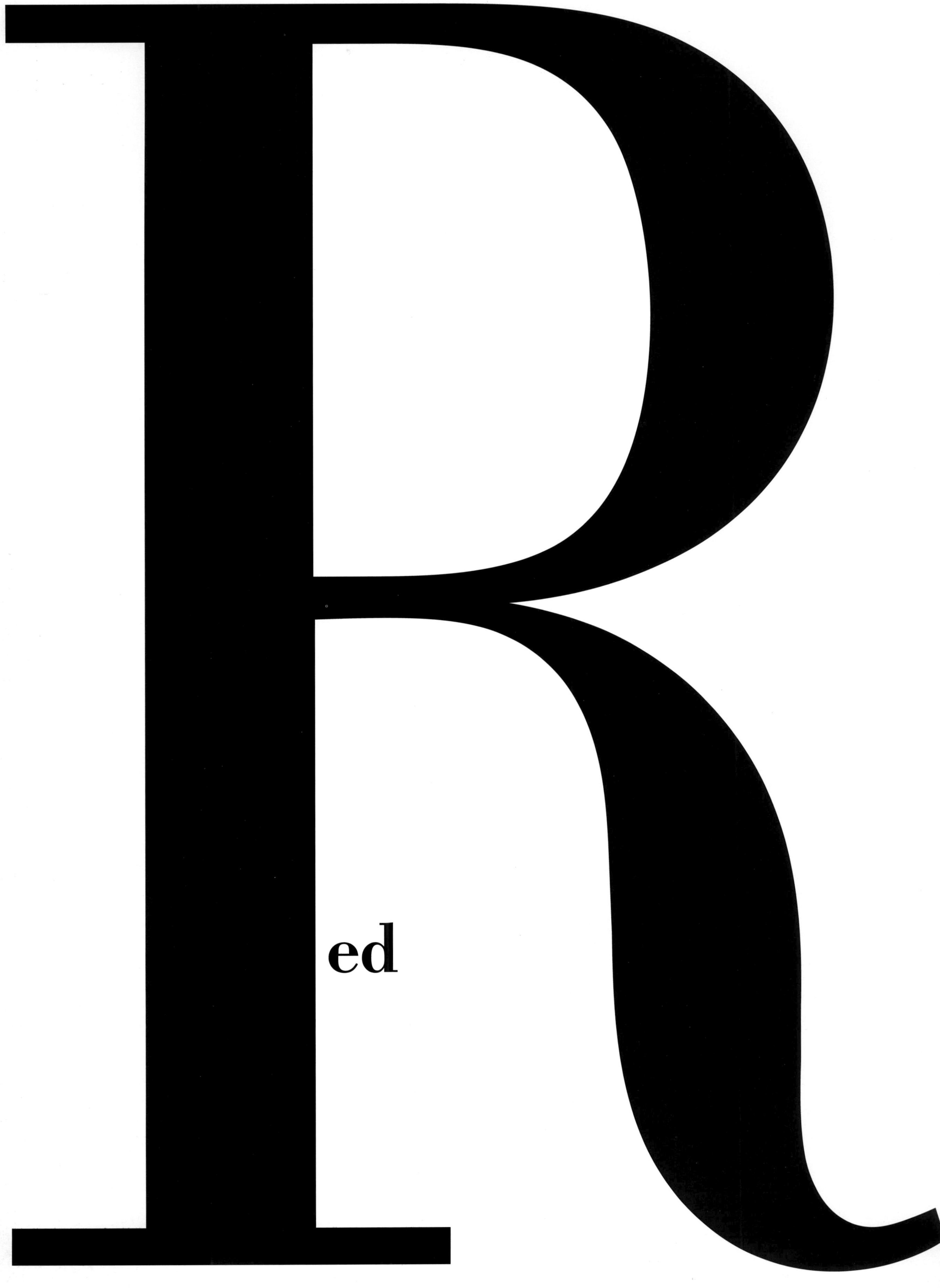
Red

Page 57
Couture. Spring–Summer 1965.
Empire line in "Valentino red," a dress that made history with its architectonic neckline and draped front.
Rome, Accademia Valentino.
Photo Janos Grapow/Archivio Valentino.

"Why so much red? Perhaps because I was born under the sign of Taurus? In any case, red is a bewitching color, standing for life, blood, and death, passion, love, and an absolute remedy for sadness and gloom. I remember one of the most striking impressions I ever had in my life: it was in Barcelona, when I was a student. I'd been invited by a friend of mine to the opera where with fascination I beheld, in a box, a very beautiful greyhaired woman dressed in red velvet from head to toe. Amid all the colors worn by the women, she appeared to me to be unique, standing out in all her splendor. I have never forgotten her. For me she became the red goddess. Something fabulous. I think a woman dressed in red is always magnificent. In the middle of a crowd, she is the quintessence of the heroine. Diana Vreeland continues to be for me the greatest heroine of all times. She had an acute sense of things, of true fashion. She had an infallible critical eye. She knew better than anybody else the meaning of the word *allure*, she was also a great journalist. And then, she also adored the color red; her apartment was completely *rouge*. Unique!"

Couture. Fall–Winter 1988–89.
Red crêpe evening gown heavily draped around the bodice and the sleeves, with flowing chiffon scarf edged in matching satin.
Drawing Mats Gustavson/Archivio Valentino.

Page 55
Diana Vreeland, the "fashion goddess", photographed in front of her portrait by William Acton.
Photo Jonathan Becker/Grazia Neri.

WOLF
FORM CO.
N.Y.C.

Rome, Via Gregoriana.
1960. Valentino in his atelier with highlights of red in the décor.
Photo Team/Grazia Neri.

Couture. Spring–Summer 1959.
Low-cut red tulle evening gown
with drapery of red roses over a balloon skirt.
Photo Courtesy *Harper's & Queen.*

Page 60
Rome, Atelier Valentino.
1983. Jerry Hall before the show,
wearing the clothes and jewelery of the collection.
Photo Barry McKinley.

Boutique. Fall–Winter 1988–89.
Paris. "Ecological" fake fur in "Valentino red."
Photo Robert Frankenberg/*Marie Claire* © Mondadori Press

Valentino red. **1.** Couture. Fall–Winter 1984–85. Evening gown with long sleeves and asymmetrical drapery.
2. Couture. Spring–Summer 1985. Evening gown with low-cut back, clinging fit, and two black taffeta bow accents.
3. Couture. Spring–Summer 1983. Pleated and long-fringed evening gown.
Photos Janos Grapow/Archivio Valentino.

Valentino red. **1.** Couture. Spring–Summer 1989. Slinky evening gown with asymmetrical neckline and short, draped petal-sleeve.
2. Couture. Fall–Winter 1984–85. Slinky evening gown with vertical drapery and fitted sleeves.
3. Couture. Fall–Winter 1987–88. Evening gown in damask fabric with black ribbon insert ending in a large bow.
Photos Janos Grapow/Archivio Valentino.

Boutique. Fall–Winter 1991–92.
Red wool crêpe suit.
Photo Mario Testino/Courtesy *Harpers' & Queen*.

Page No. 358.

Boutique. Spring–Summer 1991.
Coral crêpe toga worn over a low-cut white crêpe pant suit and coral embroidery in a floral pattern.
Photo Steven Meisel.

Page 68
Boutique. Fall–Winter 1992–93.
Red dress with red satin bow at the back.
Photo Luigi Volpe/Courtesy *Madame Figaro*, 1992.

"In fantasy color becomes a story, a succession of images. When that color is red and the image is created by clothing" the storyteller is Valentino. The article of clothing in red—or better, in "Valentino red"—is something more than a way of telling a story: it is synonymous with style and therefore out of the ordinary. Red is a constant feature of Valentino's fashions, a note that is not only chromatic, but a flash of great allure, of elegant seduction. Each time it appears, Valentino red is like a leitmotiv in the continuing symphony of each of his défilés. Contemporary, timeless, infinitely varied, Valentino red undergoes a process of self-detachment. Valentino red is a given fact, a reality outside of current events; it is closer to the idea of the myth. Valentino explains: "I started to fall in love with this color during my first visit to Barcelona when I was seventeen years old. A friend took me to the opera; it was the start of the season. The women perched in the boxes around me seemed to be a garland of red flowers. They all wore something in red, and it struck me. That image came back to me when I started designing." The memory can be traced back to one of the first dresses that a very young Valentino designed for a famous friend when he was still in the atelier of Jean Dessès in Paris. The line was romantic, conceived for an elegant figure, where the red is exalted by the play of transparency, the contrast between lustrous and matte, with ribbon and knot motifs. This elegant evening gown already shows the essence of Valentino's style: a style that never ceases to astonish, to amaze, though it still respects the rules of the game. It is a classical look that harks back to various canons. Innovating in response to creative needs, the rigorously composed styles alternate with other more opulent, baroque styles where a fundamental role is played by the selection of a fabric with the right values in a sort of eclecticism ranging between the world of the present and the illusion of a past. The unquestionable craftsmanship blended with the study of detail always yields stunning results. We know that red is a stimulating color; it is synonymous with warmth and energy; it is also the symbol of strength and passion; it is eye-catching, rousing, and contagious. Red is one of the three primary colors, and one that most lends itself to *sfumato.* It has always had strong, though at times contradictory, symbolic values, representing love, but also violence. In Christian iconography red stands for spiritual greatness often linked to martyrdom, but its ambivalent nature enabled it to become in medieval painting a symbol of the inferno, the color of the demon. Red can be a disturbing key to the interpretation of such folklore classics as "Little Red Riding Hood," where it stands between innocence and seduction. With Valentino, red is also the red of his favorite poppies which are a recurrent motif in the print fabrics he uses. This flower's petals are a pretext, a point of departure in his creations; they can be transformed into a dress blown by the wind, an ethereal material such as voile or chiffon. Each era has recurrent images that reflect its aesthetic, becoming metaphors, allegories, embodying utopias and ambiguities; all this surfaces in the image of the period's "fashion". An example is Valentino red; in fact, "lovers of consummate beauty," aesthetes, elegant people of culture appreciate the message of Valentino red, especially in our times of colorful though insistent messages. Discerning the beauty of "detail," avoiding "conspicuous waste", and giving rise to sensations that stand out for the quality and subtlety of their formal rigor—this is beauty for beauty's sake, a complete abstraction. Red is red because it is Valentino.

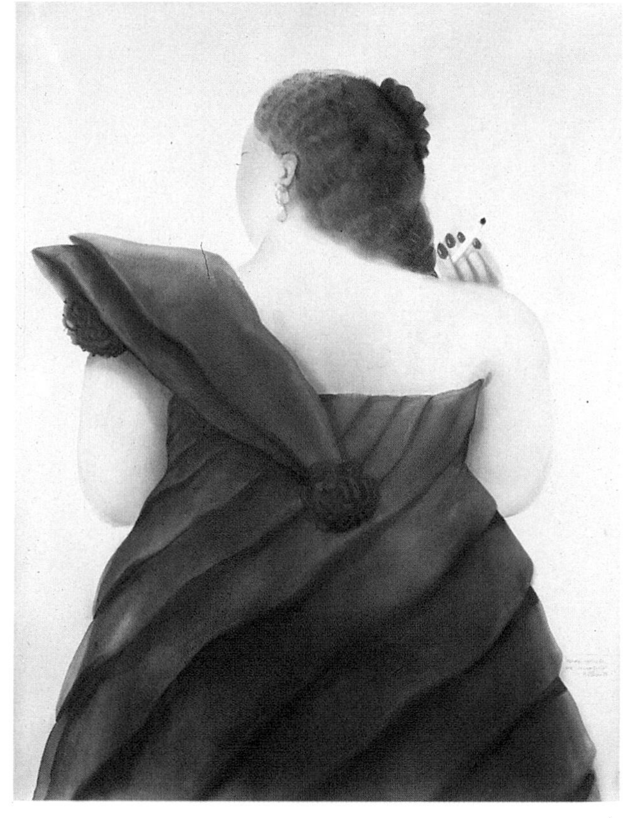

Fernando Botero, *Femme habillée en Valentino.*
Oil on canvas, 47 x 40 in.
Rome, Valentino Garavani collection.

Page 71
Couture. Fall–Winter 1988–89.
Evening dress in red crêpe and chiffon, classical line.
Photo Walter Chin/Archivio Valentino.

Bonizza Giordani Aragno

Couture, Spring/Summer 1981
Brooke Shields wearing a [illegible] evening gown inspired by Botero's *Femme habillée en Valentino.*
Photo Dick Ballarian/Courtesy *Harper's Bazaar Italia.*

1989. Jewelry, eyeglasses, gloves, and stole.
Photo Gary Deane.

Page 75
Valentino red rose.
Photo Russel Lamb.

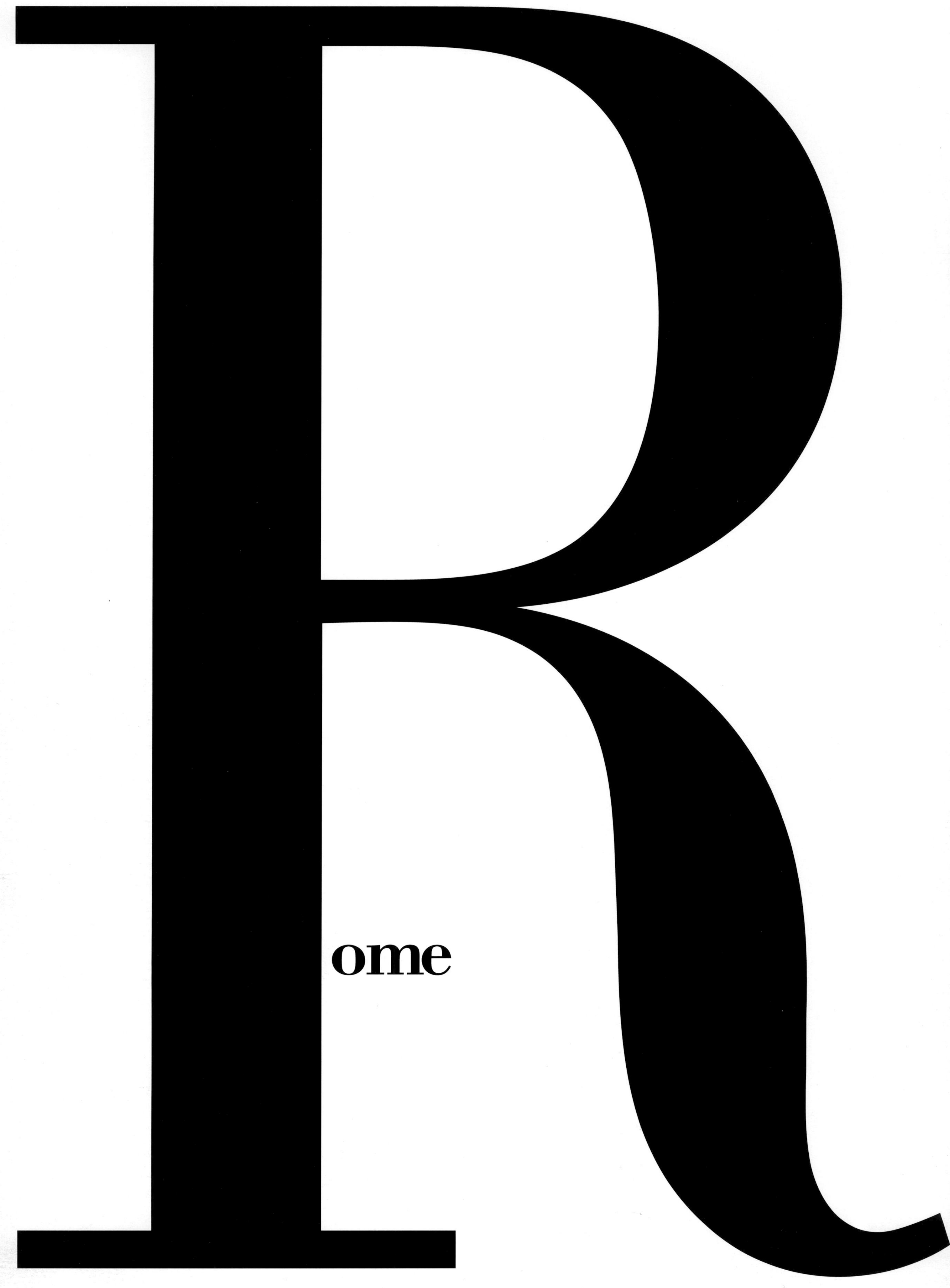
Rome

“Rome is unique: a city where one should not work, but only walk about, seeing the sights and discovering new things all the time. It’s a city that takes my breath away. When in Rome, one should take the opportunity to experience the *Ponentino*, at that magical hour between day and night, when gentle relaxation at last takes over. It is a city of lights, of co-

lors. It’s the city of love—indeed, it is a love affair that never grows stale. Rome is a delightful mistress who makes us feel that we, too, are eternal.”

Couture. Spring–Summer 1972.
Valentino at the Imperial Forum.
Photo Herbert Rowan/Archivio Valentino.

Page 77
Rome. View of the Imperial Forum under a blanket of snow.
Photo Isidoro Genovese.

Page 79
Couture. Fall–Winter 1984–85.
Draped black velvet dress with black jersey jacket. Fur cuffs and hat.
Photo Arthur Elgort/Courtesy *Vogue* © 1984 Edizioni Condé Nast S.p.A.

Couture. Spring–Summer 1976.
An encounter between baroque architecture and fashion in Rome's Piazza del Popolo. Wool chain-printed coat.
Photo Regi Relang. Courtesy Verlag Hans Schöner
© *30 Jahre Mode Italien.*

Page 81
Couture. Fall–Winter 1984–85.
Evening dress with draped bodice in pink silk jersey and a matching silk skirt in Rome's via Condotti.
Photo Mark Arbeit/*Moda.*

Couture. Spring–Summer 1980.
Black crêpe evening dress
with large white taffeta bow.
Photo Alberta Tiburzi.

Page 83
Couture. Spring–Summer 1980.
Yellow crêpe de chine evening gown
with matching taffeta bows.
Rome, Monument to the Unknown Soldier.
Photo Alberta Tiburzi.

Boutique. Spring–Summer 1995.
Claudia Schiffer in a beige chiffon-and-organza crinoline dress
with embroidered skirt and bodice.
Photo Arthur Elgort/Archivio Valentino.

1985.Valentino celebrates twenty-five years of fashion with his Couture seamstresses on Piazza di Spagna's steps. Photo Jean-Paul Goudeaut.

My first 10 years

rotosei

settimanale

Rossana Podestà nell'atelier del sarto Valentino (Servizio alle pagine 48-51)

2
3
4
7
6
8
9
13
10
11
14
15

2
3
4
5
6
7
8
11
Page @No. 358.
12
13
14
15

B
elles
de jour

“When I dream of preparing my collection, my immediate thought is of an evening dress; if the concept of work comes into the picture, then I think of a daytime outfit. That's because it's much easier to imagine a woman walking across a ballroom than an active type who has to get through the whole working day and emerge triumphant. The daytime part of a collection calls for a lot of technical research; it's a very important part because it represents the hallmark, the essential character of a fashion parade. The ‘Belle de Jour’ has to be even more remarkable because hers in an environment of less artifice. The daytime beauty needs to display her self-confidence unflaggingly for a great many hours on end. That's why I feel it's up to me to give her a carefree image.”

Page 97
Couture. Fall–Winter 1983–84.
Wool houndstooth jacket with asymmetrical lapels over a black velvet dress; small toque with feather.
Photo Horst P. Horst/Courtesy *Vogue* © 1983 Edizioni Condé Nast S.p.A.

Page 98
Boutique. Spring–Summer 1970.
Blue wool redingote over blue-and-white printed silk dress.
Photo Oliviero Toscani/Archivio Valentino.

Boutique. Fall–Winter 1990–91.
Red wool coat cinched at waist with a small self-belt.
Photo Michel Comte/Courtesy *Vogue* © 1990 Condé Nast Publications Inc.

Haute Couture. Spring-Summer 1985.
Pink wool jacket with double row of black buttons.
Photo Stan Malinowsky.

Haute Couture. Fall-Winter 1963-64.
Pink wool suit with bow at waist; jaguar hat.
Photo Archivio Valentino.

Prêt-à-porter. Fall-Winter 1990-91.
Short pink wool coat with jewel neckline.
Photo Patrick Demarchelier/Courtesy *Vogue*
© 1990 Edizioni Condé Nast S.p.A.

Couture. Fall–Winter 1966–67.
Trouser suit in tweed wool; fur and fabric hat.
Photo Helmut Newton/Courtesy *Vogue* © 1966 Edizioni Condé Nast S.p.A.

Boutique. Fall–Winter 1981–82.
White spencer with black velvet buttons and collar; black trousers.
Photo Claus Wickrath/*Donna*.

Page 104
Boutique. Checked wool suit and white silk shirt.
Photo Max Vadukul/Courtesy *Vogue*

Boutique. Fall–Winter 1986–87.
Black cashmere jewelneck sweater with rhinestone embroidery on the sleeves; a chiffon scarf with the same motif is wrapped around the model's head.
Photo Denis Piel/Courtesy *Vogue*

Boutique. Fall–Winter 1988–89.
Blue shantung dress with white lapels and large buttons down the middle.
Photo David Bailey/Courtesy *Vogue*
© 1988 Edizioni Condé Nast S.p.A.

Couture. Fall–Winter 1965–66.
Op-striped blue-and-white suit with solid-color collar and pockets.
Photo Archivio Valentino.

Couture. Fall–Winter 1987–88.
Seven-eights camel hair coat.
Photo Giampaolo Barbieri.

Boutique. Spring–Summer 1991.
White shantung suit.
Photo Jacques Olivar/Courtesy "Marie Claire Italia"

1. Couture. Fall–Winter 1987–88. Red cashmere redingote edged in sable. Photo Vittoriano Rastelli/Archivio Valentino.
2. Couture. Fall–Winter 1985–86. Quilted jacket with fur trim. Photo Terence Donovan/Archivio Valentino.
3. Boutique. Fall–Winter 1989–90. Blue spencer over a gray quilted skirt open in front; blouse with lace collar, reminiscent of the nineteenth century. Photo Walter Chin/Archivio Valentino.
4. Florence, Palazzo Pitti. Couture. Fall–Winter 1963–64. Shocking pink wool suit. Photo AIS.
5. Boutique. Fall–Winter 1987–88. Black suit with velvet collar and jewerly by Valentino. Photo Steven Meisel/Archivio Valentino.
6. Couture. Fall–Winter 1988–89. Brown suit with pleated skirt, blouson-style jacket with broad collar and cuffs in fur, man's-style hat. Photo David Bailey/Archivio Valentino.

Page 111
Couture. Spring–Summer 1995.
Black wool gabardine suit; straight skirt and jacket with trapezoidal neckline and braid buttons.
Photo Courtesy *Joyce.*

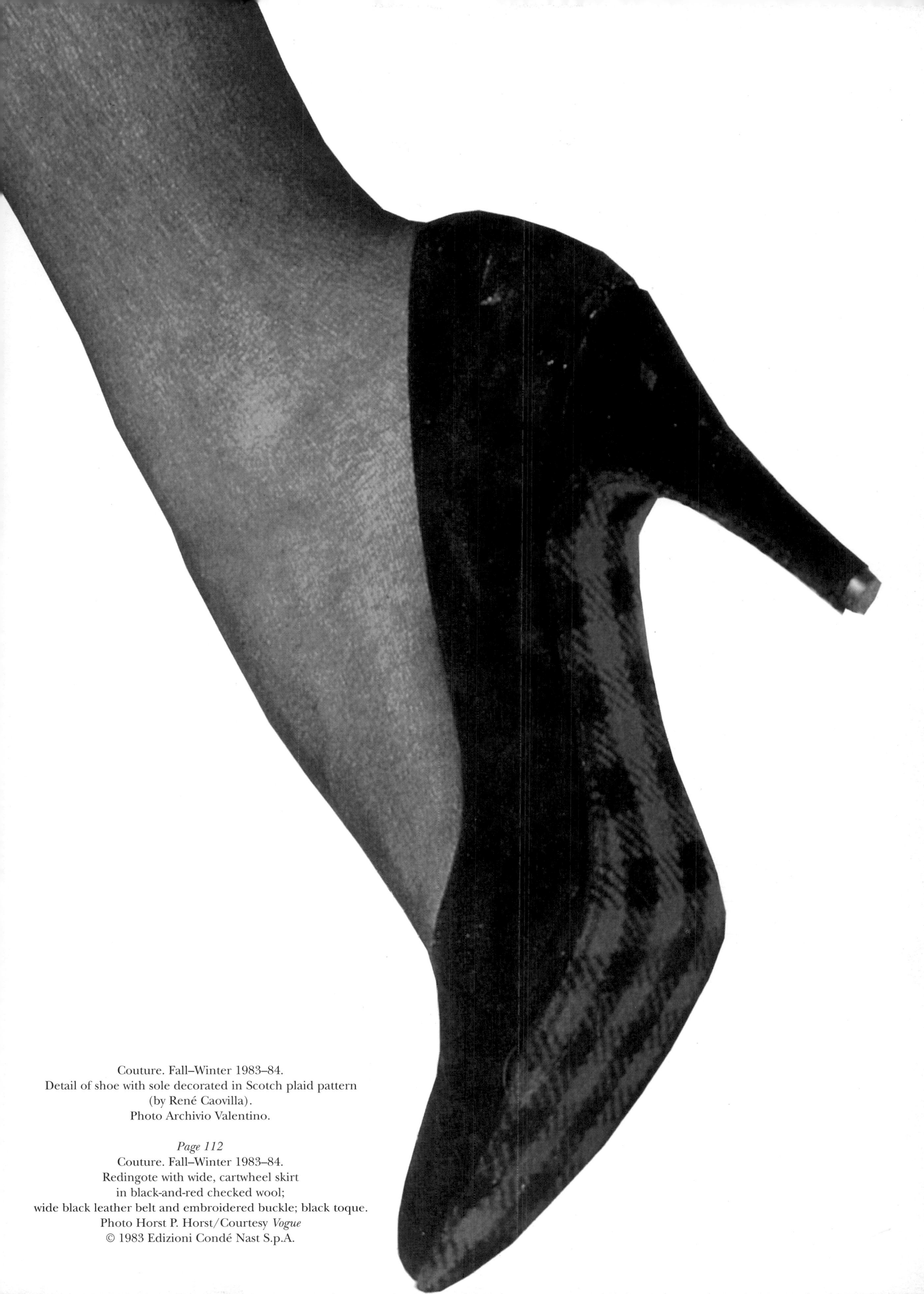

Couture. Fall–Winter 1983–84.
Detail of shoe with sole decorated in Scotch plaid pattern
(by René Caovilla).
Photo Archivio Valentino.

Page 112
Couture. Fall–Winter 1983–84.
Redingote with wide, cartwheel skirt
in black-and-red checked wool;
wide black leather belt and embroidered buckle; black toque.
Photo Horst P. Horst/Courtesy *Vogue*

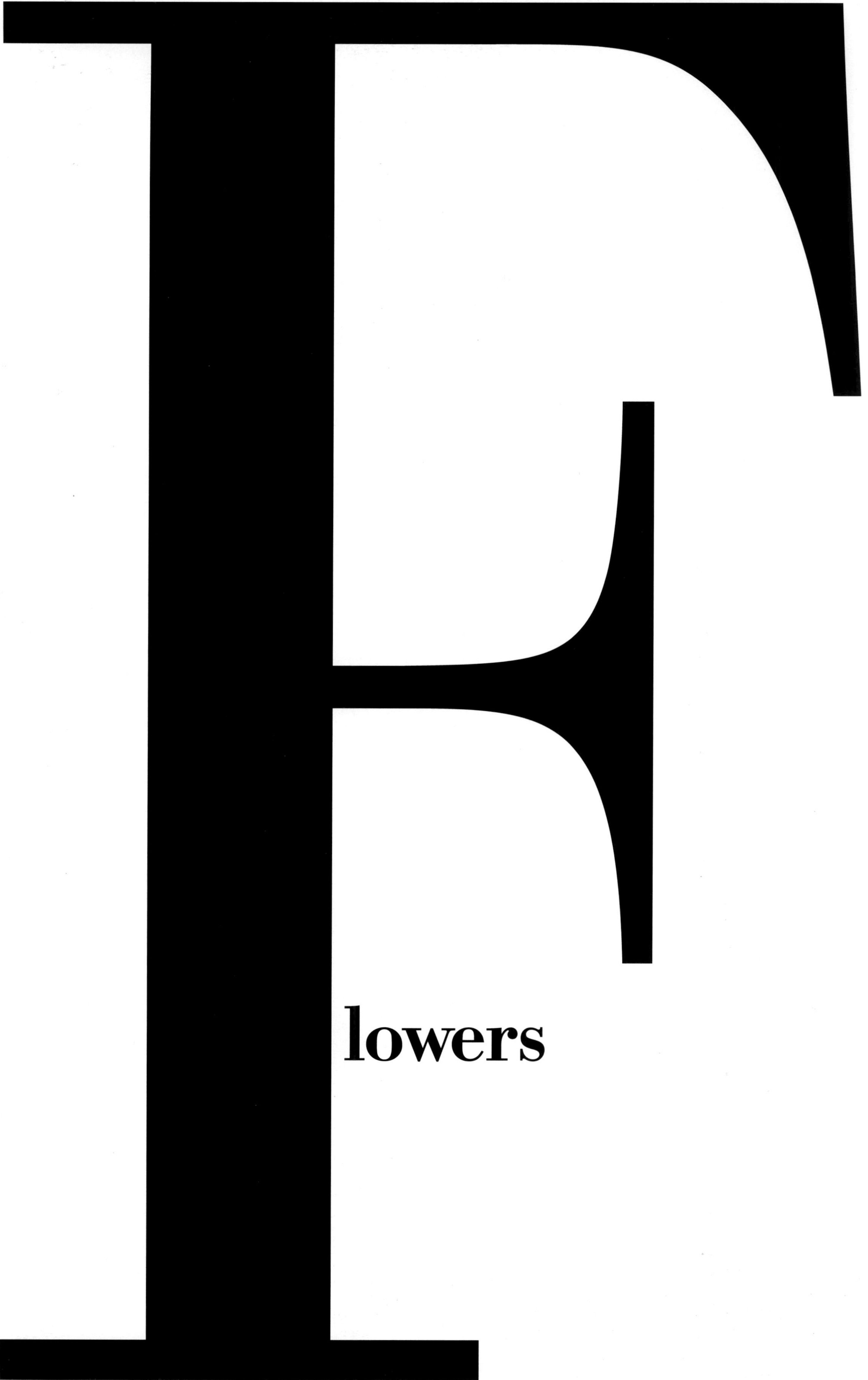
Flowers

“I shouldn’t like to go through life without flowers. I love being surrounded by them; so often, they are a sign of joy. None of houses can be without them. Sometimes I buy them myself—in fact, one of my greatest pleasures is to go out and buy some at Covent Garden market. Flowers, for me, are a great source of inspiration; I like to reproduce them on a dress, turning a woman into a bouquet. They bring happiness. I have a passion for peonies; I always look for a very big, spectacular one that comes from San Francisco. I think I must be a true collector of these ephemeral works of art. I also like roses, cyclamens, snowballs, pink camellias, and hibiscus. I have paid homage to all these flowers that overwhelm me with their beauty in my creations of fabrics and dresses.”

Page 115
Paris, Jardin de Bagatelle.
Photo Alexandre Bailache/Archivio Valentino.

Page 117
Couture. Spring–Summer 1969.
White evening dress with floral motifs embroidered in petit point.
Photo Carlo Orsi.

Page 118
Detail of bolero with sequin and rhinestone embroidery.
Photo Janos Grapow/Archivio Valentino.

Page 119
Couture. Fall–Winter 1989–90.
Evening dress in flower print satin with flowing satin stole.
Photo Walter Chin/Archivio Valentino.

C[illegible] Giancarlo Giammetti's country ho[illegible] [illegible]ail of the [illegible]ter garden[illegible]
Pho[illegible] Oberto Gil[illegible] *Ho[illegible]se & [illegible]arden*

F.M. Ricci
BRANCUSI

Couture. Spring–Summer 1986.
Flower print dress with draped bodice.
Drawing Michael Meyring.

Page 122
Couture. Spring–Summer 1968.
Organdy dress with embroidered flowers and pleated cuffs, embroidered stockings, eighteenth-century-style shoes with bow.
Photo Regi Relang/Courtesy Verlag Hans Schöner
© *30 Jahre Mode Italien.*

Couture. Spring–Summer 1989.
Victorian-style flower-print silk evening gown with drapery and ruche trim at the waist and along the edges.
Venice, Museo Fortuny.
Photo Cristina Ghergo/Archivio Valentino.

Couture. Fall–Winter 1991–92.
Pink satin bag with floral design.
Photo Tyen/Archivio Valentino.

Boutique. Spring–Summer 1991.
Black and white silk-satin dress with stiff gauze petticoats.
Photo Giovanni Gastel/Courtesy "Donna"

lack
and white

“A woman dressed in black and white is to me like a kind of symbol or a signature. In all my collections I always include a black-and-white item, because it provides a sort of rest in the middle of all the colors. At the same time, this kind of punctuation interrupts and thus strengthens a collection. Black and white is just as much a classic as red or beige. A woman who wears black and white is strong and certain to have a great personality—a woman who knows what she wants. That's the sort of woman I admire.”

Couture. Fall–Winter 1989–90.
Black stretch leggings with sweeping black and white satin stole.
Photo Satoshi Saikusa/Courtesy *Vogue*
© 1989 Edizioni Condé Nast S.p.A.

Page 129
Victor Vasarely, *Helios*, 1960.
Oil, 77 x 86 in.
Paris, Galerie Denise René.

Page 131
Couture. Fall–Winter 1967–68.
Veruschka. Palazzo pajama in oversized black polka-dot pattern.
Photo Franco Rubartelli/Courtesy *Vogue*
© 1967 Edizioni Condé Nast S.p.A.

Couture. Fall–Winter 1979–80.
Mask inspired by surrealism.
Photo Courtesy *Harper's Bazaar Italia.*

Page 132
Drawing from the book *Ornament zwischen Hoffnung und Verbrechen,*
by Josef Hoffmann, Vienna 1987.
Photo Archivio Valentino.

1
2
3
4
5
Page No. 358.
6
7
8
9
10
11
12
13

Boutique. Spring–Summer 1990.
Long, striped sheath-dress
in black-and-white crêpe marocain.
Photo Alfa Castaldi/Courtesy *Vogue*

Boutique. Fall–Winter 1990–91.
Black-and-white houndstooth check wool coat; quilted velvet hat.
Photo Neil Kirk/Courtesy *Vogue House* © 1990 Edizioni Condé Nast S.p.A.

Page 136
Boutique.
Pleated silk pants with diagonal black and white stripes.
Photo courtesy *Madame.*

Spring–Summer 1987.
Black-and-white Valentino outfits.
Photo Gary Deane/Archivio Valentino.

Page 139
Couture. Fall–Winter 1965–66.
Sequined top with op-inspired geometrical motifs.
Photo Janos Grapow/Archivio Valentino.

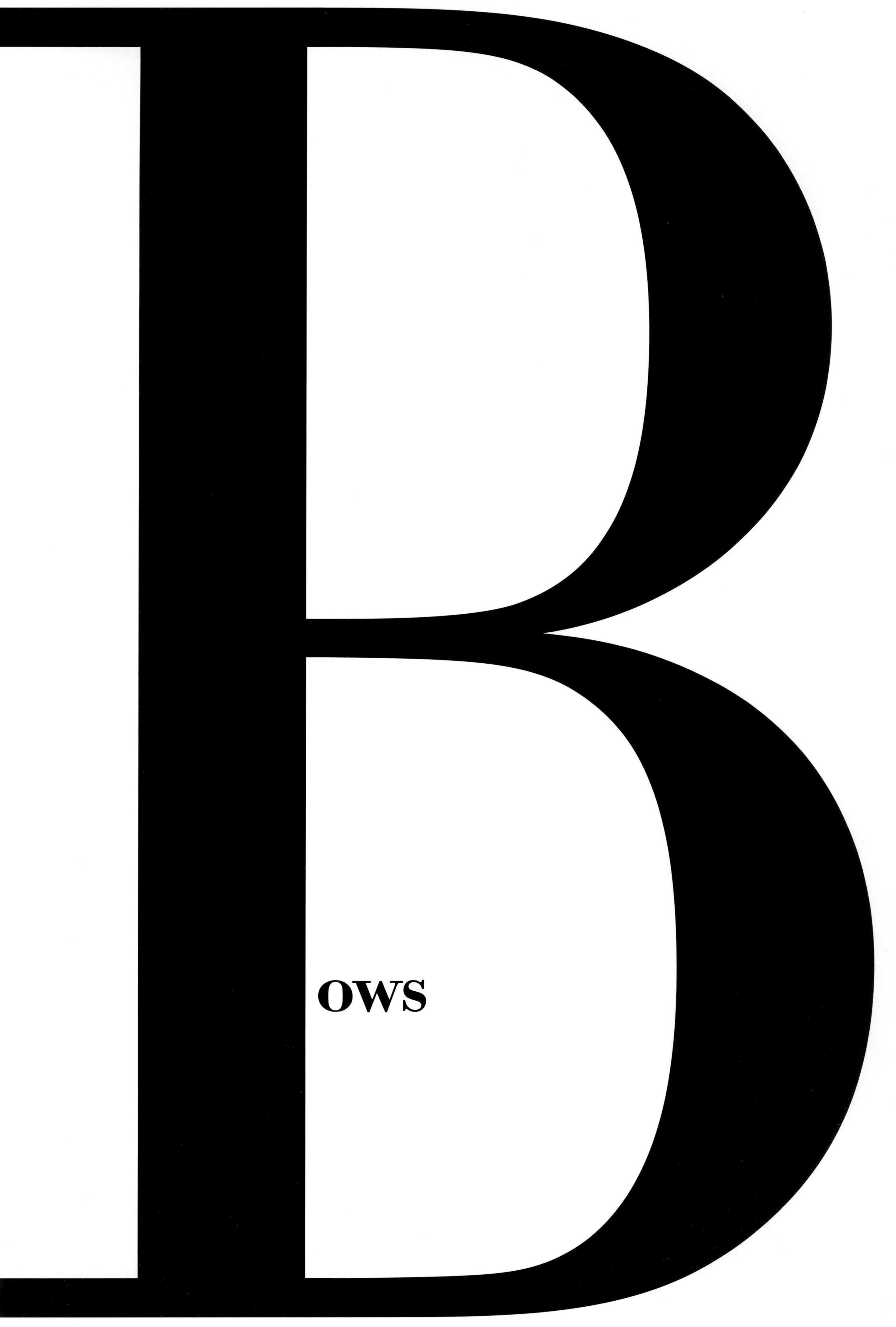

Bows

“ Bows are an obvious symbol of total femininity. As indispensable as an exclamation point at the end of a phrase, they may be a refined way of marking the spot where draped materials cease to flow. They remind me of one of my favorite models: the famous Dalma who during a fashion parade presented a red dress that ended in a bow. The people clapped for ten minutes, and she dissolved in tears. It was one of my most rewarding moments. ”

Couture. Fall–Winter 1985–86.
Baroque-look bracelet with double bow
in gemstones and rhinestones.
Photo Bob Stern.

Page 141
Couture. Fall–Winter 1987–88.
Detail of pink satin skirt with ruffle hem and large bow;
shoes in matching pink satin.
Photo Javier Vallhonrat/Studio Filomeno.

Page 143
Boutique. Spring–Summer 1991.
Low-cut dress in black shantung with large white bow at the wais
black polka-dotted white underskirt and straw hat.
Photo Steven Meisel/Archivio Valentino.

Couture. Spring–Summer 1983.
Detail of evening dress with large butterfly bow
at the back in black-and-white printed fabric.
Photo Renato Grignaschi/Archivio Valentino.

Page 144
Boutique. Fall–Winter 1988–89.
Heavy black satin evening dress
with three large white bows.
Photo Walter Chin/Archivio Valentino.

Page No. 359.

Boutique. Fall–Winter 1985–86.
Long red sheath-dress with drapery clasped by a looped black bow.
Photo Philippe Webb/ *L'Officiel.*

Page 147
Couture. Fall–Winter 1989–90.
Detail of black jacket with three embroidered bows in different colors.
Photo Serge Barbeau/ *L'Officiel.*

Page 149
Couture. Spring–Summer 1996.
Long white silk crêpe dress with embroidered belt and bow at one side.
Photo Walter Chin.

Boutique. Fall–Winter 1987–88.
Black evening gown with pleated underskirt in the same gold fabric as the looped ribbon.
Photo Nadir/Courtesy *Vogue* © 1987 Condé Nast Verlag GmbH.

Page 151
Couture. Fall–Winter 1982–83.
Richly draped black evening gown with bow clasp at the waist and a large rose in its center.
Photo Arthur Elgort/Courtesy *Vogue*
© 1982 Les Publications Condé Nast S.A.

1

2

4

6

7

8

9

10

Page No. 359.

Boutique, Spring–Summer 1980.
Evening gown with oversized bow.
Photo Peter Lindbergh/Courtesy *Vogue*

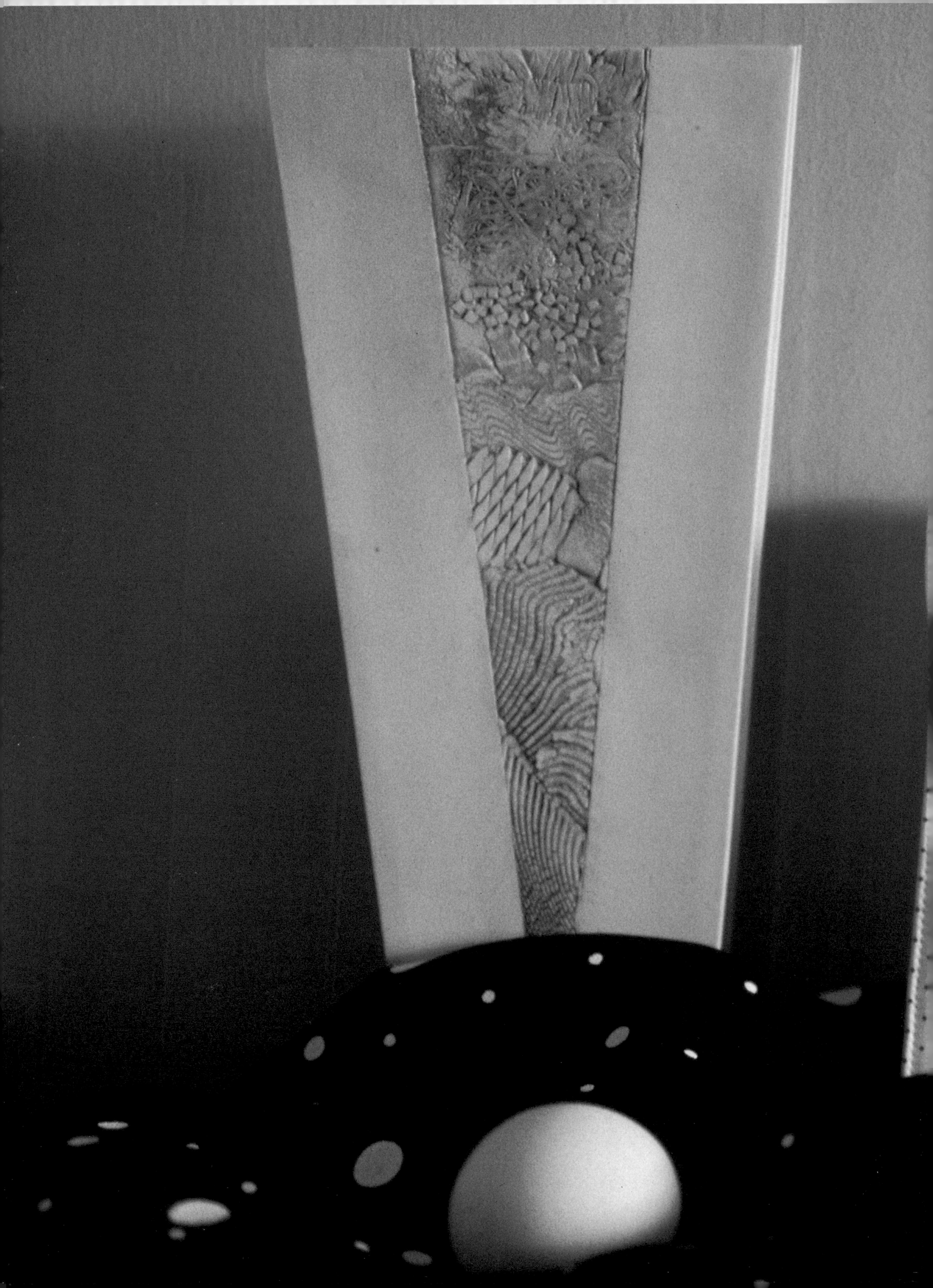

Boutique. Spring–Summer 1985.
A galaxy of large and small polka dots
on a tightly fitted dress.
Photo Sheila Metzner/Archivio Valentino.

Pages 158-159
Clutch bag in rigorous geometric lines
with tiny polka dots pattern.
Photo Sheila Metzner/Archivio Valentino.

Couture. Spring–Summer 1988.
Black silk and black-and-white polka-dot satin evening gown.
Photo David Bailey/*Amica*.

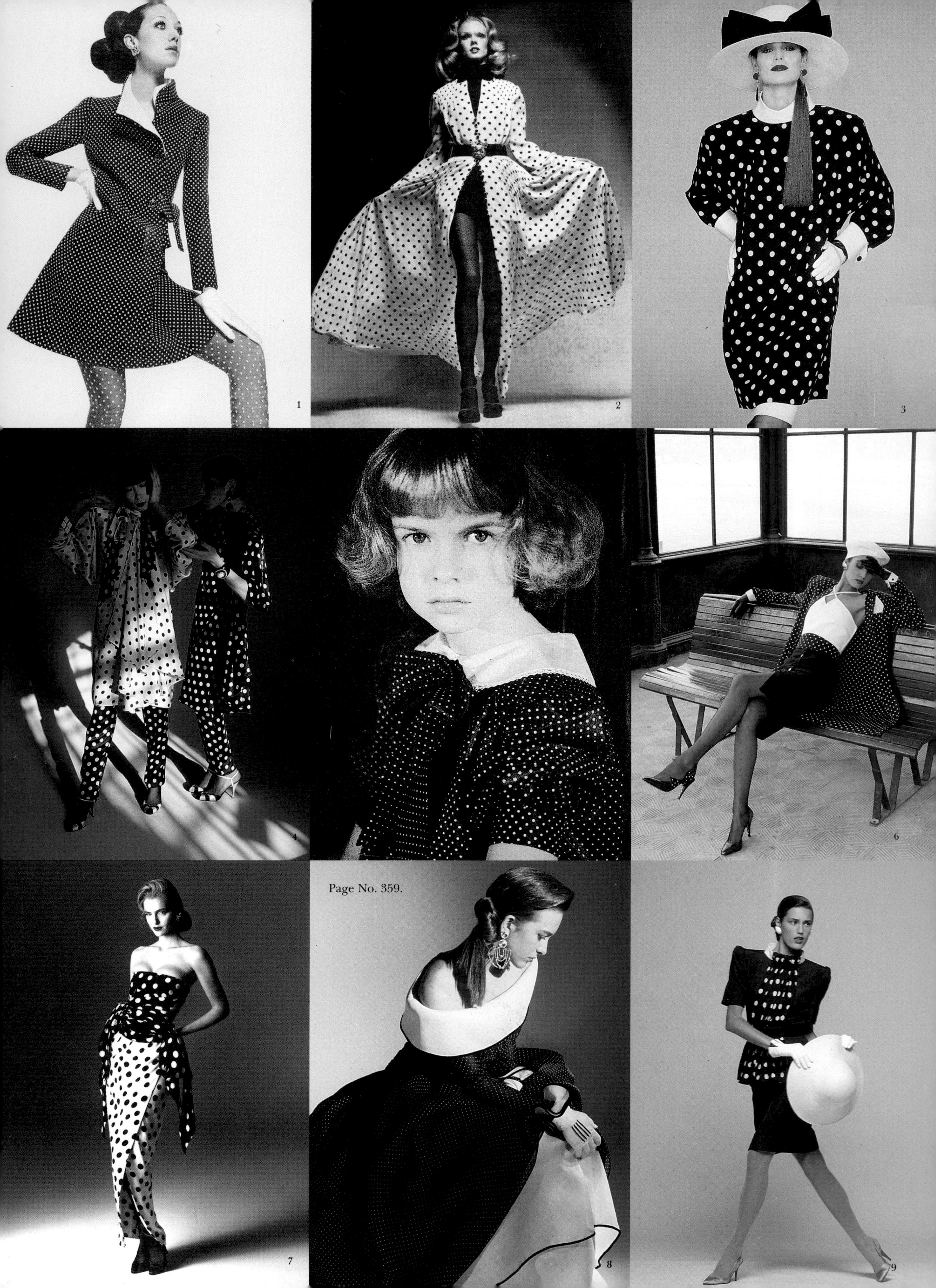
1
2
3
4
6
Page No. 359.
7
8
9

Boutique. Spring–Summer 1984.
Evening gown with black and white sequin polka dots.
Photo Alberta Tiburzi.

Shoe. 1985.
Polka dots and scalloped edging in classic shoe design.
Photo Jim Reiher/Archivio Valentino.

Page 164
Boutique. Spring–Summer 1992.
Black polka-dotted white silk dress
with side slit and black lace undershirt.
Photo Peter Strube/*Elle* U.K.

Boutique. Spring–Summer 1987.
Red chiffon dress in red-and-black polka dots;
turban with large bow and black rose.
Photo Lothar Schmidt/Archivio Valentino.

Page 167
Boutique. Spring–Summer 1988.
Detail of petal-shaped sleeve in floral pattern silk
with oversized polka dots.
Photo Courtesy *Harper's Bazaar Italia.*

From the sea

SUSAN WOOD

“The sea holds me in its spell almost more than anything else because I find it impossible to resist its infinite, everchanging beauty. For it has the magic and the strength of the mountains, which are also dear to my heart. I love its many colors, its poetry, and its calm. Mankind should heed and respect it, instead of filling it with all kinds of harmful refuse.”

Boutique. Spring–Summer 1983.
Bathing suit with large appliqué wave.
Photo Giovanni Gastel/*Donna.*

Page 169
Valentino Più, 1974.
Shell-shaped pillows.
Photo Susan Wood.

Page 171
Valentino 1984.
Draped bathing suit with rhinestone ring.
Photo Helmut Newton/Archivio Valentino.

Pages 172-173
Scipione, *Il risveglio della bionda sirena* (*The Blond Siren's Awakening*), 1929.
Oil on panel, 31 1/2 x 39 in. Archivio della Scuola Romana.
(Exhibited at the opening of the Accademia Valentino
on January 18, 1990.)

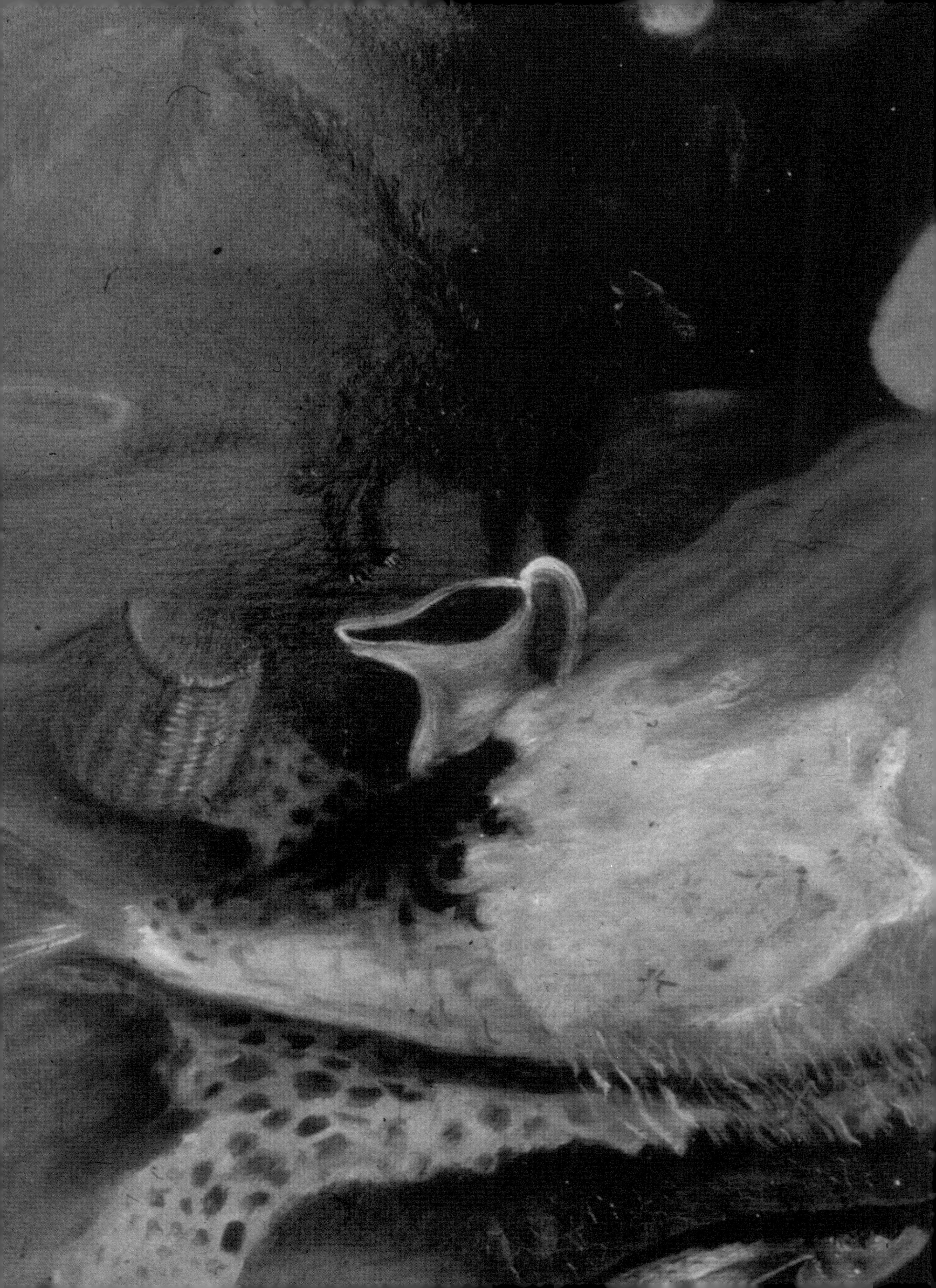

Boutique. Spring–Summer 1984.

Boutique. Spring–Summer 1991.
Low-cut white crêpe pant suit with sequin embroidery and beaded coral branches and appliqué shells.
Photo Christian Moser/Courtesy *Vogue*.

Boutique. Spring–Summer 1993.
Claudia Schiffer in a black bathing suit
and rhinestone-studded sunglasses.
Photo Arthur Elgort/Archivio Valentino.

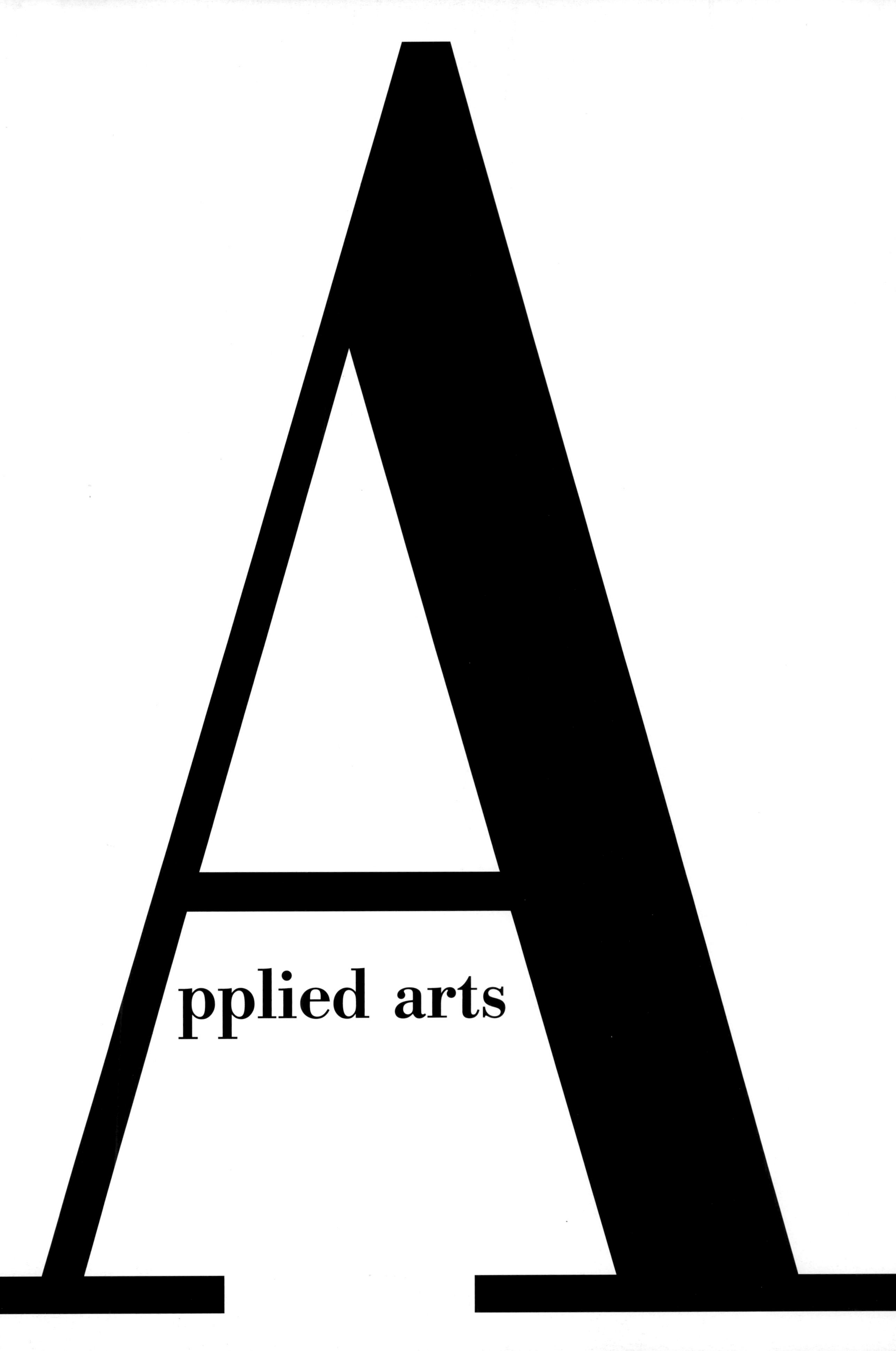
Applied arts

Amphora. Second half of the sixth century B.C.
Black-figured attic vase, height 12 in.
Rome, Museo Nazionale Etrusco di Villa Giulia
(formerly Castellani Collection).
Photo Archivio Valentino.

Page 187
Boutique. Fall–Winter 1989–90.
Sweater embroidered with motifs inspired by Etruscan pottery.
Photo Janos Grapow/Archivio Valentino.

ΑΙΝΕ

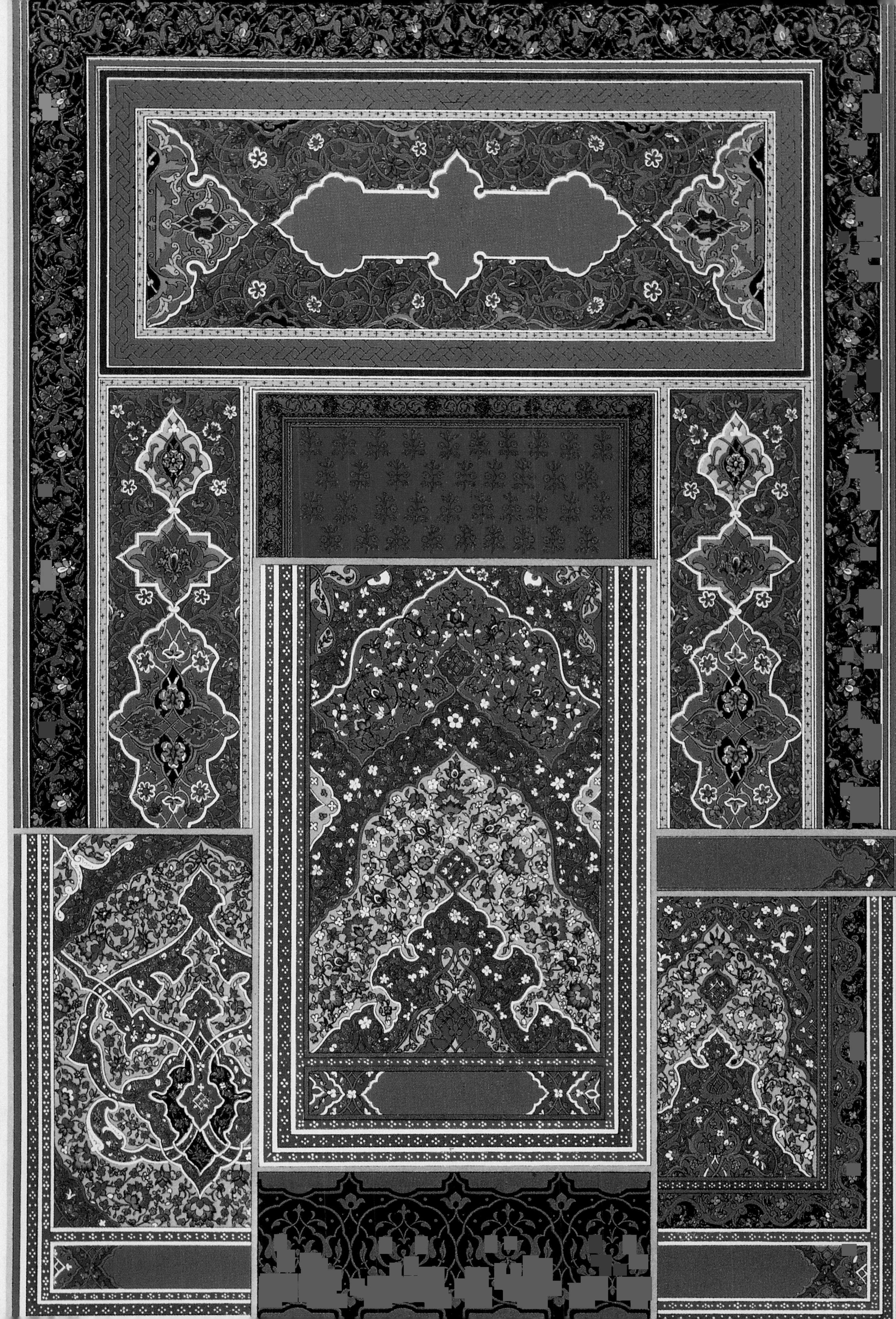

Couture. Fall–Winter 1989–90.
Black-and-white satin evening gown
with decorative motif
inspired by Hoffmann.
Photo Cristina Ghergo/Archivio Valentino.

Page 188
Rembrandt, *The Polish Horseman.*
New York, Frick Collection.

Page 189
Couture. Fall–Winter 1969–70.
Red wool coat with sable fur trim.
Photo Marc Hispard.

Page 190
Coin from Massalia.
Paris, Bibliothèque Nationale.

Page 191
Couture. Spring–Summer 1990.
Ball gown with embroidered top
using motifs inspired by Bruges lace.
Photo Cristina Ghergo/Archivio Valentino.

Page 192
Couture. Spring–Summer 1965.
Pleated chiffon palazzo pajama
and heavy silk coat.
Photo Archivio Valentino.

Page 193
Indo-Persian miniature.
Photo Archivio Valentino.

Page 194
Josef Hoffmann and Kolo Moser,
Interior of the Maison de couture Flöge,
Vienna, 1904.
Photo Archivio Valentino.

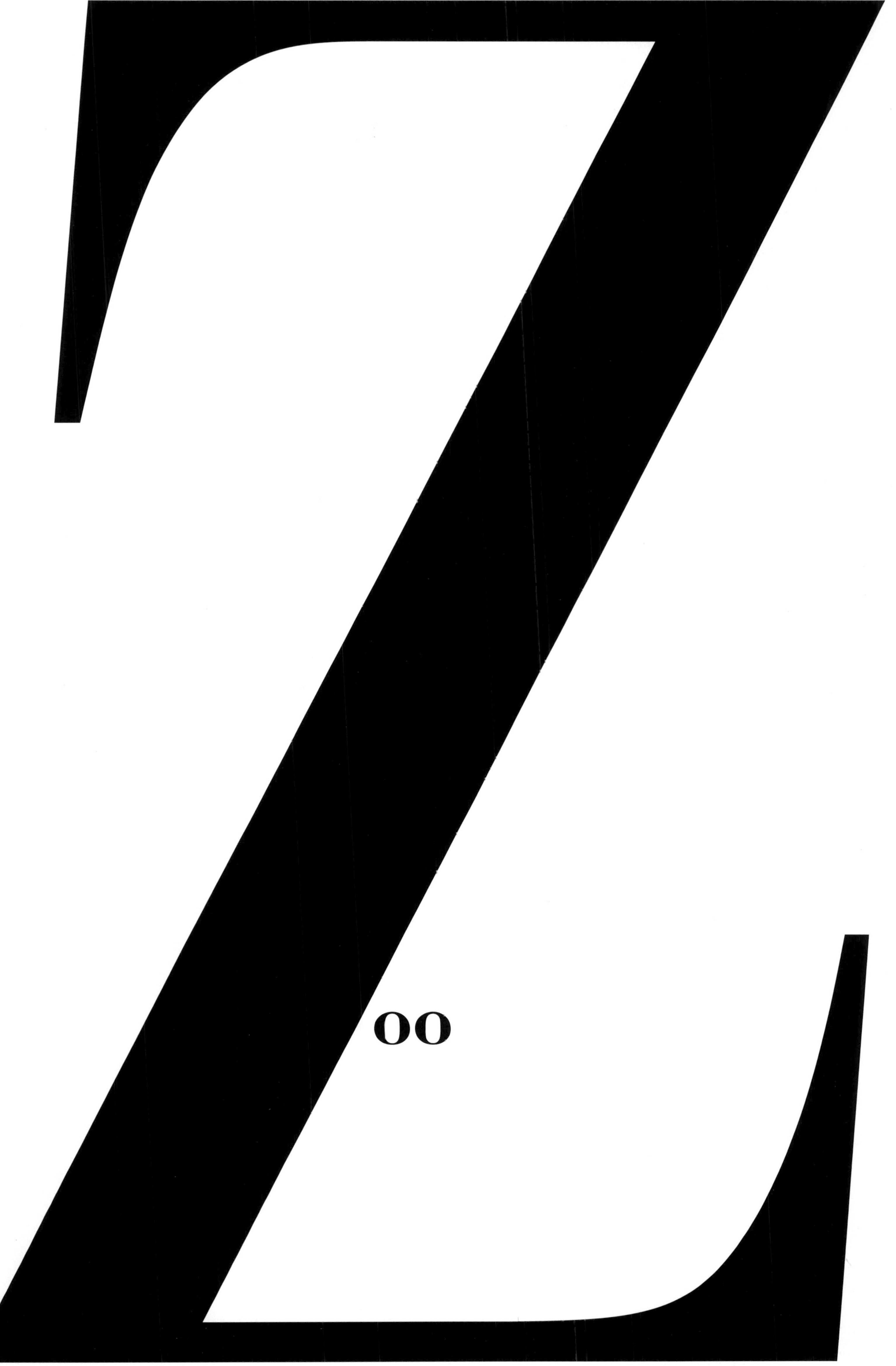
Zoo

"At the start of my career, when haute couture was indulgent and, with its wealthy clients, was able to be as bold as it liked, I had some crazy ideas: an ermine coat lined with leopard, lynx capes, the first white mink coat, in the seventies. Extravagance, at whatever cost, was the order of the day. Then we had qualms of conscience and began to feel some sense of responsibility. Knowing that the natural world was endangered and that the massacre of animals was avoidable, why should we continue to kill them? As far back as 1962 I had invented a black and white fake zebra and in 1965 crocodile prints. So I took up the motif of animal prints, which I consider a happy stylistic innovation, a sort of divertissement that lets the imagination run free. Nevertheless, I remain firmly convinced that a woman should feel absolutely free to choose among various possibilities what she wants to wear, following her own taste and her own sensibility, and not the more or less ideological decisions made presumptively by others."

Close fitting dress in white wool crêpe with cashmere scarf in leopard print.

Page 198
Couture. Fall–Winter 1988–89.
Les Sacs. Bag in leopard print.
Photo David Bailey/Archivio Valentino.

Page 201
Couture. Spring–Summer 1966.
Palazzo pajama with cotton tunic in giraffe print.
Photo Archivio Valentino.

Page 202
Boutique. Spring–Summer 1988.
Evening dress with chiffon zebra-motif leggings.
Photo Alberta Tiburzi.

Page 203
Boutique. Spring–Summer 1988.
Chamois zebra-motif glove.
Photo Archivio Valentino.

Page 204
Couture. Fall–Winter 1990–91.
Leopard-motif embroidered evening jacket.
Photo Janos Grapow/Archivio Valentino.

Page 205
Boutique. Dress in leopard print voile.
Photo Jouanny Christophe/Courtesy *Anna*.

Pages 206-207
Couture. Spring–Summer 1970.
Beige midisuits in leopard-print cotton.
Photo Oliviero Toscani.

Couture. Fall–Winter 1969–70.
Trouser suit with maxi overcoat
in double-face wool with python motif.
Photo Giampaolo Barbieri.

Page 208
Couture. Fall–Winter 1992–93.
Long gloves with leopard-motif embroidery.
Photo Christian Moser/Courtesy *Marie Claire*
© 1992 Mondadori Press.

Page 210
Couture. Fall–Winter 1987–88.
Detail of sequin embroidery in tiger motif.
Photo Janos Grapow/Archivio Valentino.

Page 211
Couture. Fall–Winter 1967–68.
Tiger-motif wool coat and trousers
with black jersey tunic.
Photo Franco Rubartelli/Archivio Valentino.

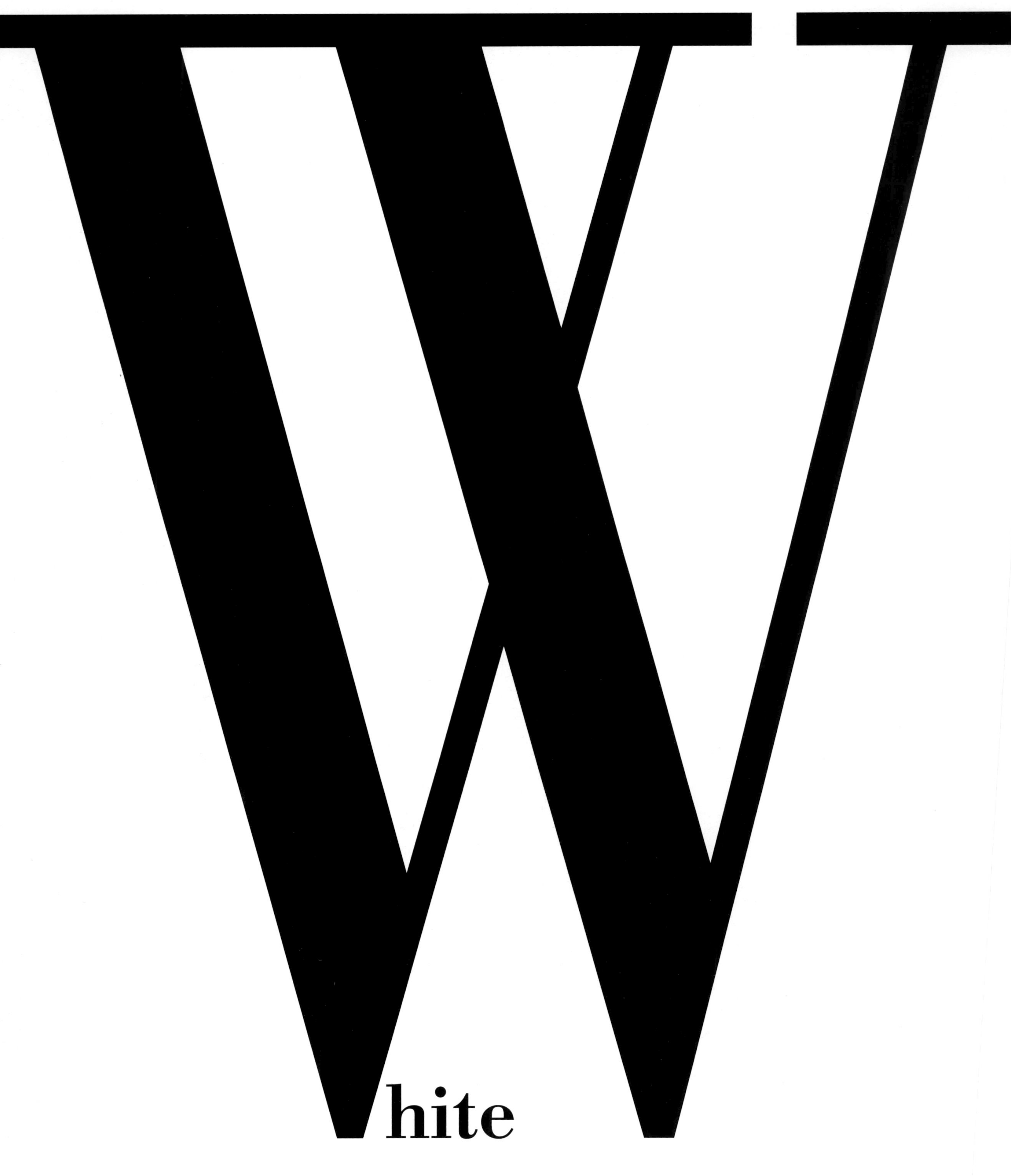

hite

Couture. Fall–Winter 1968–69.
White chiffon embroidered dress
with ostrich feather trim.
Photo Giampaolo Barbieri.

Page 223
Couture. Spring–Summer 1968.
White cotton evening suits with pearls
and rhinestones embroidery.
Photo Henry Clarke/Courtesy *Vogue*

Couture. Fall–Winter 1968–69.
White wood coat with cock's feather trim on edges and hem.
Photo Giampaolo Barbieri.

Folk

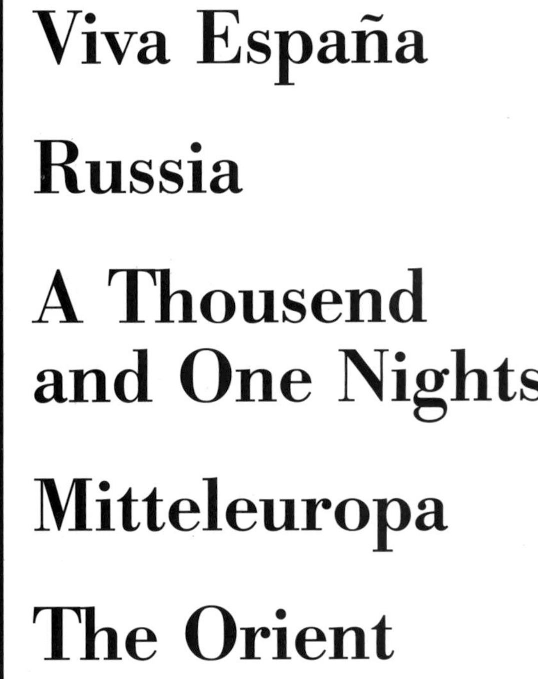

Viva España

Russia

A Thousend and One Nights

Mitteleuropa

The Orient

“Traveling always stimulates desires; or rather, the desire to travel moves me to depict the images that various countries may produce. The inspiration that the world offers me is unlimited, but over the years the way of expressing it has completely changed. I hate the period around 1970, because all fashion designers, including myself, wer too close, too faithful to the themes that inspired us. Nowadays I know that I react like a painter: I am freer, more detached, vis-à-vis such influences. Nevertheless, all manner of things may attract me: Hungary, Bavaria in Ludwig's day, China, or some kitschy show I happened to see in a faraway land. But the result will not so closely resemble the thing that inspired it.”

Page 227
Collage.
Atelier Valentino.
Photo Janos Grapow.

Page 229
Couture. Spring–Summer 1997.
Kimono-cut coat in hand-painted silk.
Photo Steven Meisel.

Pages 230-231
Couture. Fall–Winter 1983–84.
Sequin-encrusted evening dress
with black jet bead fringe.
Photo Gary Deane.

Couture. Spring–Summer 1997.
Sheath dress with American-style neckline in organza embroidered with iridescent beads in floral patterns.
Photo courtesy *Elle France.*

Page 233
Boutique Fall–Winter 1997–98.
Gold lamé dress with embroidered flowers.
Photo K. Taira/Courtesy *Amica* © 1997.

Couture Uomo/Donna. Fall–Winter 1969–70.
Donna: ample cape and fur hat, "Anna Karenina" style,
with fur trim. Uomo: maxi overcoat with fur hat.
Photo Francesco Scavullo.

Page 235
Couture. Fall–Winter 1983–84.
Fur accessories and rhinestone jewelry.
Photo Giampaolo Barbieri.

Couture. Spring–Summer 1988.
Gem dress. Mini torero's bolero
and little dress in black silk crêpe
with openwork rhinestone embroidery.
Photo David Bailey/Archivio Valentino

Page 237
Boutique. Spring–Summer 1991.
White silk crêpe trousers
with American Indian motifs.
Photo Dominique Issermann/*Vanity Fair.*

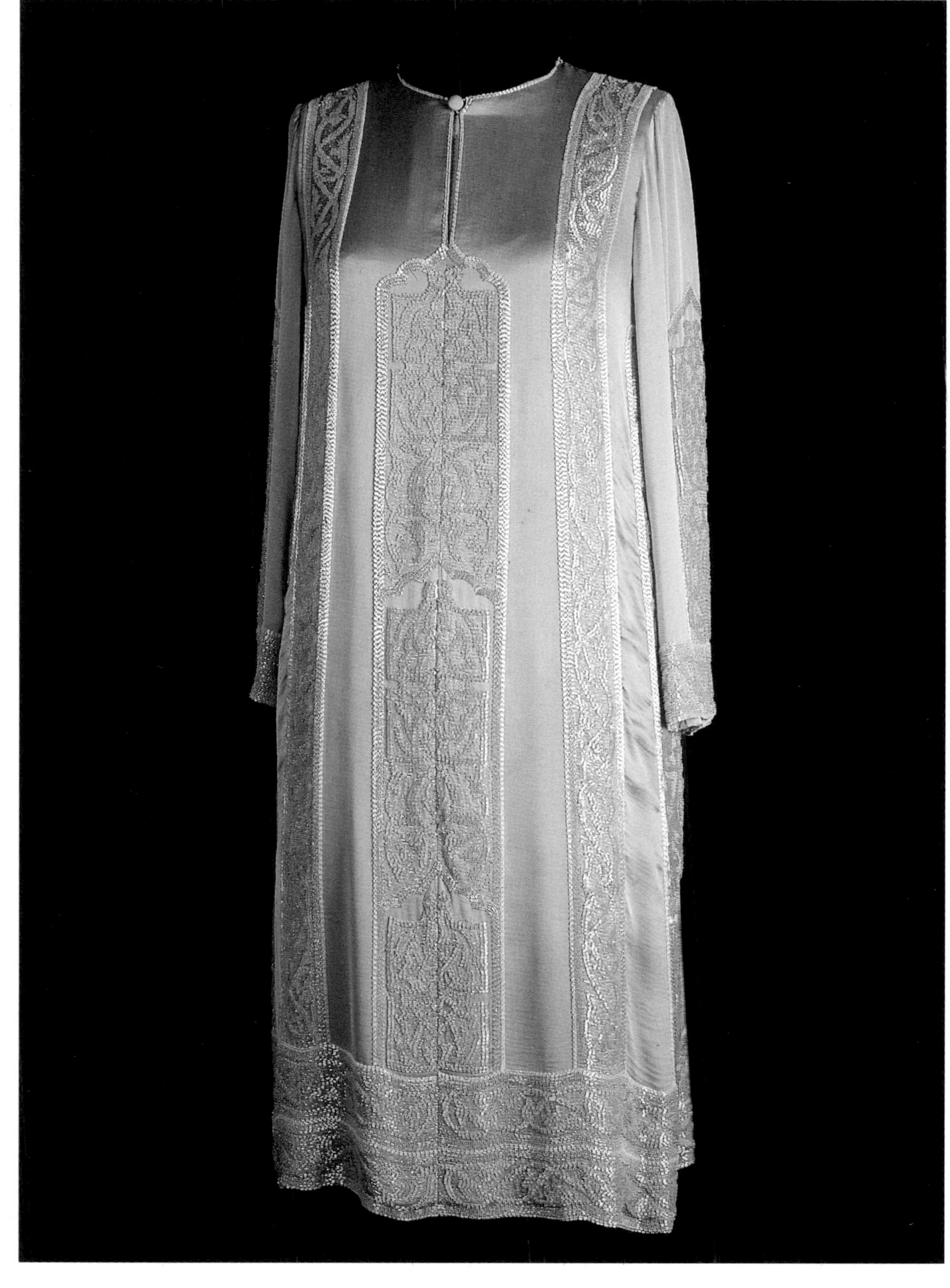

Couture. Spring–Summer 1976.
Embroidered tunic with motifs taken from mosque mosaics.
Photo Janos Grapow/Archivio Valentino.

Page 238
Boutique. Fall–Winter 1983–84.
Brown lamé evening gown inspired by oriental painting.
Photo Barry Lategan/Courtesy *Vogue* © 1983 Condé Nast Verlag GmbH.

Boutique. Fall–Winter 1977–78.
Group photo with clothing inspired by Ludwig of Bavaria.
Photo Deborah Turbeville/Archivio Valentino.

Arab-inspired harem trousers
with African-style accessories.
Left, belt with African-inspired buckle.
Photos Nicolas Bruant/Archivio Valentino

Couture. Fall–Winter 1965–66.
Palazzo pajama: fabrics with Indian
and Indonesian motifs,
coral and gemstone accessories.
Photo Elsa Haerter/ *Grazia* ©
Mondadori Press.

Boutique. Fall–Winter 1970–71.
Maxidress with fabric inspired by Turkish folk motifs.
Photo Irving Penn/Courtesy *Vogue*
© 1970 Condé Nast Publications Inc.

Page 246
Boutique. Spring–Summer 1990.
Embroidered chiffon top. Silk trousers with sunburst pleats.
Photo Claus Wickrath/Courtesy *Donna*.

Page 247
Couture. Spring–Summer 1992.
Black velvet dress with slit.
Feather hat by Philip Tracey for Valentino.
Photo Mauro Balletti/Courtesy *Vogue*
© 1992 Edizioni Condé Nast S.p.A.

Page 248
Boutique. Fall–Winter 1970–71.
Hooded dress: fabric with Persian motifs.
Photo Courtesy *Harper's Bazaar Italia*.

Fragments of elegance

Page 251
Couture. Spring–Summer 1972.
Chestnut-shaped jewelry.
Photo Bob Krieger.

"Just as I can get enthusiastic about one of those big butterflies that I like so much, I can completely fall for a woman who's dressed quite simply, but has the audacity to draw attention to herself with some small detail, thus becoming so remarkable that the way she's dressed no longer matters. Some out-of-this world detail invented by a woman will make her more important to me than one dressed up in all the colors of the rainbow, who just looks ordinary. For instance, a woman wearing a sweater who has the nerve to pin on it a handkerchief covered with sequins or colored stones can make my day. I like women who realize that something quite small can become everything."

Page 253
Haute Couture. Spring-Summer 1969.
Coral and gemstone necklaces.
Photo Giampaolo Barbieri.

Couture. Spring–Summer 1988.
Medieval-inspired jewelry.
Photo Marco Lanza/*Moda In*,
n. 4, 1988, Zanfi Editori.

Page 255
Couture. Fall–Winter 1985–86.
Crystal jewelry.
Photo Susan Lamér/
Frankfurter Allgemeine Magazin.

Couture. Fall–Winter 1982–83.
Black satin and gold leather shoes.
Photo Renato Grignaschi/Courtesy *Vogue*
© 1982 Edizioni Condé Nast S.p.A.

Page 256
Beauty-Bags 1989.
Clutch bag embossed with paisley pattern.
Photo Walter Chin/Archivio Valentino.

Boutique. Spring–Summer 1972.
Belt with large rose. Photo Frank
Horvat/Courtesy *Vogue*

Page 258
Boutique. Spring–Summer 1991.
Yellow silk dress with yellow-pink-and-purple coat.
Photo Steven Meisel/Archivio Valentino.

Page 260
Couture. Fall–Winter 1988–89.
A cascade of jewelry with chromatic interplay of different types of stones, pearls, and metals.
Photo Tyen/Archivio Valentino.

Page 262
Sandal with rhinestone buckle.
Photo Patrick Chevalier/Courtesy "Amica" © 1997.

Page 263
Couture. Fall–Winter 1992–93.
Long gloves with rhinestone embroidery.
Photo Patrick Chevalier/Courtesy *Grazia* ©1992 Mondadori Press.

Pages 264-265
Couture. Fall–Winter 1983–84. African-style bracelet.
Photo Bill Silano/Courtesy *Vogue* © 1983 Edizioni Condé Nast S.p.A.

Couture. Fall–Winter 1971–72.
An Egyptian-inspired ebony and diamond snake brooch.
Photo Oliviero Toscani.

COLLAPSIBLE
MODEL 1987
4

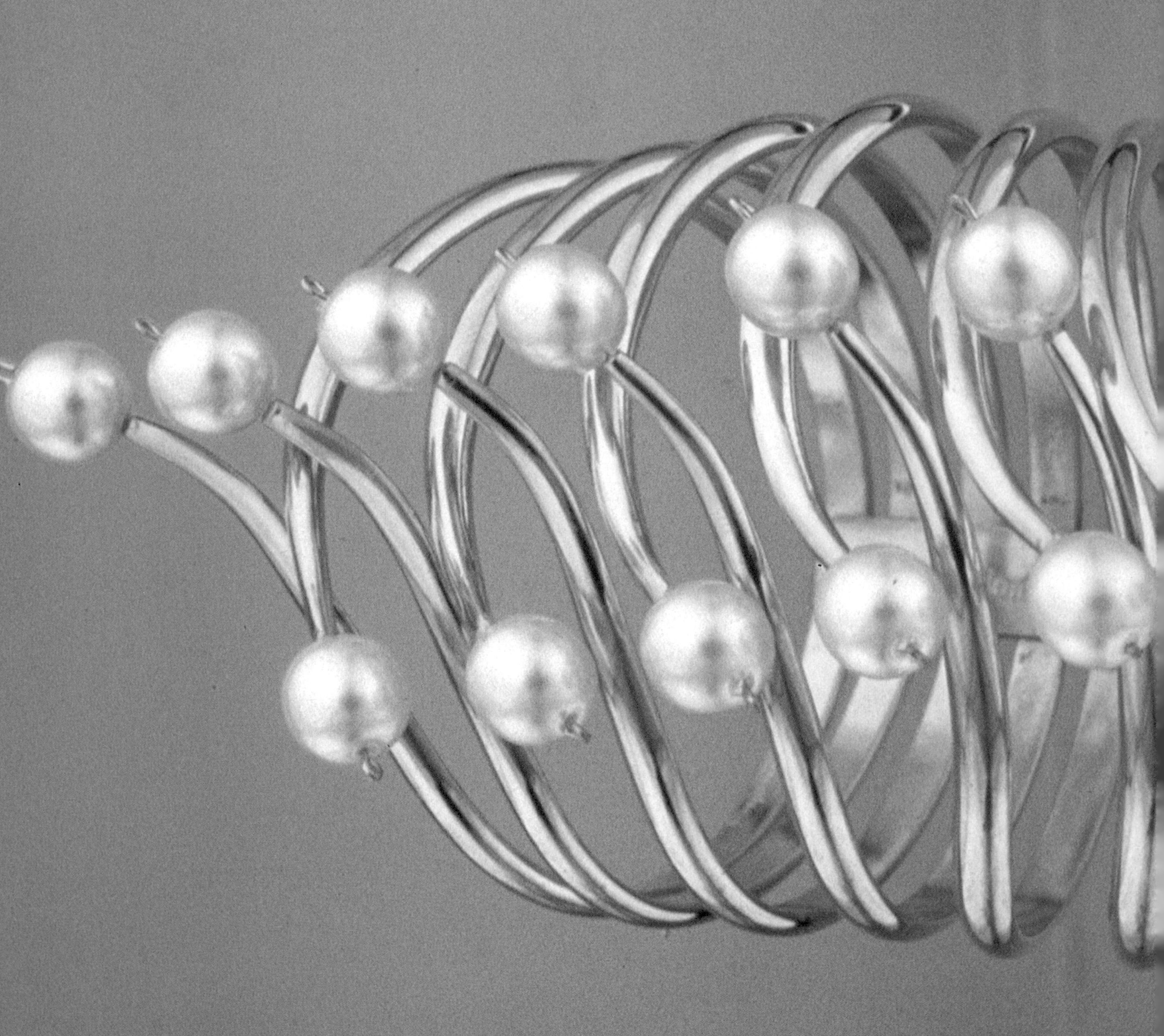

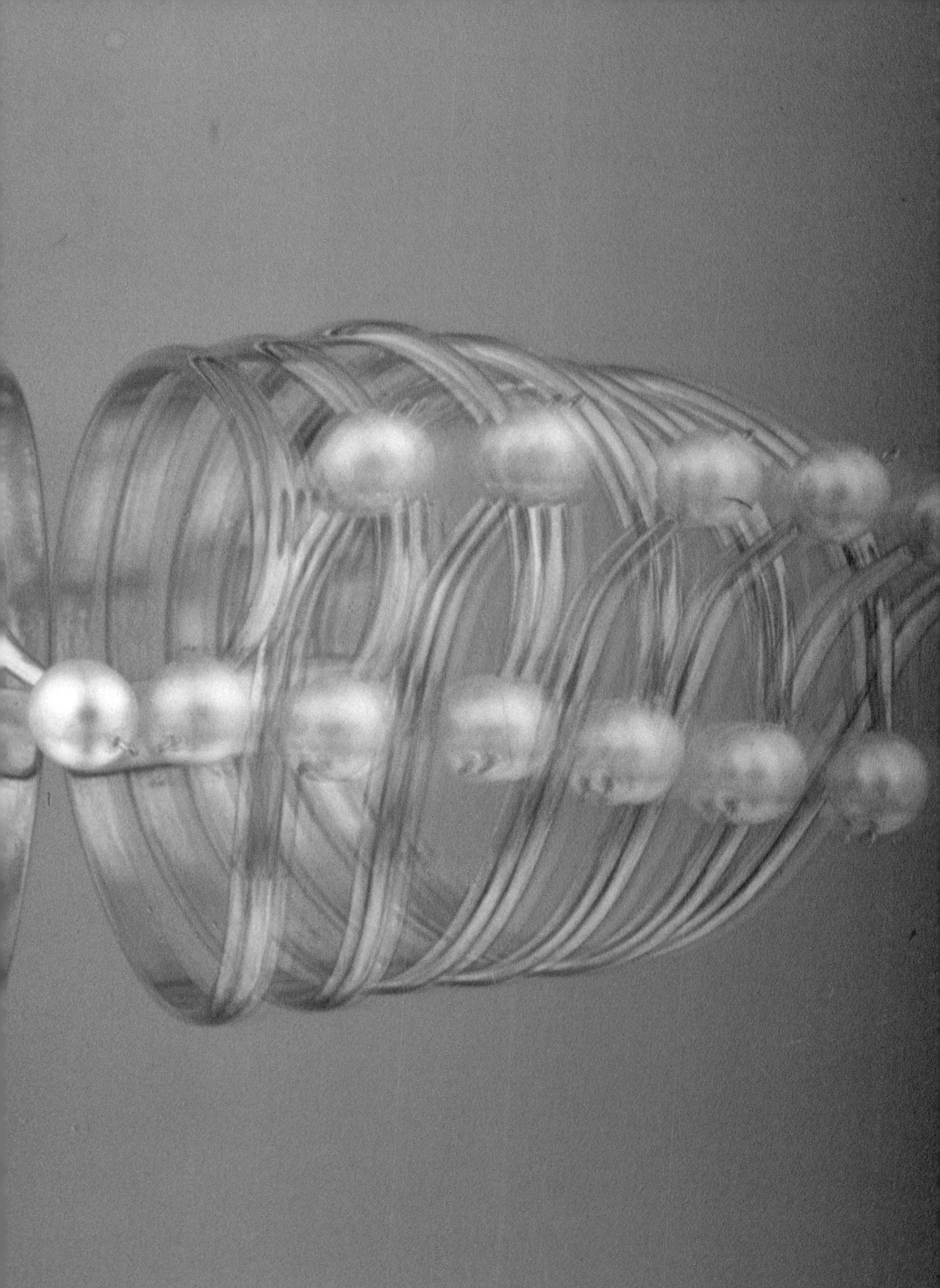

1. Couture. Spring–Summer 1963. Military style feather hat. Photo Archivio Valentino.
2. Couture. Fall–Winter 1989–90. Multi-tiered pearl necklace. Photo Serge Barbeau/*L'Officiel*.
3. Couture. Fall–Winter 1988–89. Brimmed hat with ruched ribbon band. Photo Daniel Povda.
4. Couture. Fall–Winter 1968–69. Griffin buckle. Photo Giampaolo Barbieri.
5. Couture. Spring–Summer 1987. Rhinestone and gemstone drop earrings. Photo David Bailey.
6. Boutique. Spring–Summer 1986. Rhinestone-encrusted sixties-style foulard. Photo Sergio Caminata/*Donna*.
7. Couture. Spring–Summer 1985. Crocodile clutch bag with spiral closure. Photo Jim Reiher.
8. Couture. Fall–Winter 1985–86. Cockney-style beret, decorated with pearls.
9. Couture. Fall–Winter 1989–90. Exquisite raised embroidery with diamonds and colored feathers and gemstones, of baroque inspiration. Photo Serge Barbeau/*L'Officiel*.
10. Boutique. Spring–Summer 1983. Sandals for evening wear with spiral ankle strap. Photo Alberta Tiburzi.
11. Couture. Fall–Winter 1969–70. Art nouveau snake belt. Photo David Bailey/ Archivio Valentino.

Page 266
Couture. Fall–Winter 1987–88. Embroidered tights and black satin jeweled sandal. Photo Giovanni Gastel/*Donna*.

Page 267
Couture. Fall–Winter 1988–89. Bracelet with small diamond-encrusted spheres. Photo Courtesy *Donna*.

Page 269
Couture. Fall–Winter 1987–88. Red satin embroidered shoes. Photo Albert Watson/ Courtesy *Vogue* © 1987 Edizioni Condé Nast S.p.A.

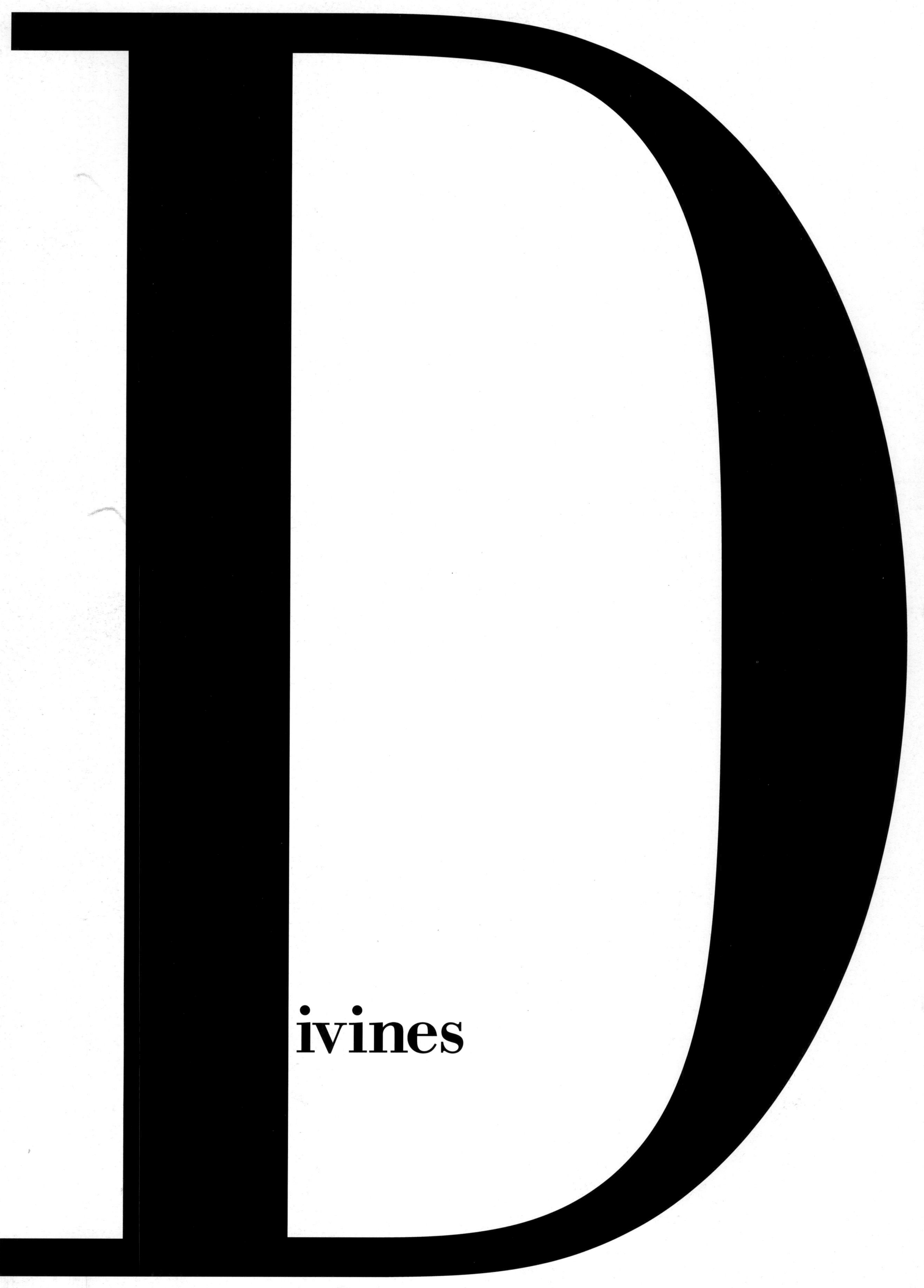
D
ivines

"*La Divine* is a dream woman. When I was young, I used to be enthralled by the great stars of the screen. That was the beginning of my boundless admiration for women of symbolic greatness such as Lana Turner, Rita Hayworth, Ava Gardner, and Marlene Dietrich. Above all, Marlene in *Seven Sinners* and Greta Garbo in *Queen Christina.* Those were the days when the masses fed on such stupendous images, feasting their eyes upon women who were sublime but beyond their reach and who inhabited a world that was somehow exalted and unreal. And so I've always cherished within me images of these untouchable women, clothed in fabulous dresses, and in pursuit of my dream I have continued to create dresses for them: my *divines.*"

Page 271
Boutique. Fall–Winter 1984–85.
Black velvet sheath-dress.
Photo Toni Thorimbert.

Page 273
Couture. Fall–Winter 1965–66.
Princess Luciana Pignatelli wearing a richly embroidered ostrich feather cape.
Photo Archivio Valentino.

Couture. Fall–Winter 1990–91.
Christy Turlington wearing an embroidered crystal motif suit.
Photo Patrick Demarchelier/Courtesy *Vogue* © 1990 Edizioni Condé Nast S.p.A.

Boutique. Fall–Winter 1987–88.
Paulina Porizkova.
Photo Arthur Elgort/Courtesy *Vogue*
© 1987 Condé Nast Publications Inc.

Couture. Fall–Winter 1988–89.
Diane de Witt.
Photo Arthur Elgort/Courtesy *Vogue*
© 1988 Edizioni Condé Nast S.p.A.

Page 277
Couture. Fall–Winter 1990–91.
Christy Turlington.
Photo Patrick Demarchelier/Courtesy *Vogue*
© 1990 Edizioni Condé Nast S.p.A.

Boutique. Fall–Winter 1977–78.
Models wearing evening gowns
in Ludwig of Bavaria style.
Photo Deborah Turbeville.

1952. Wedding gown in white lace designed by Valentino for the Wanda sisters' wedding. Photo Gary Deane.

1
2
3
4
5
6
Page No. 359.
7
8
9

Boutique. Fall–Winter 1989–90.
Paris. Black satin ball gown with bow.
Photo Henry Clarke/Courtesy *Vogue*

Page No. 359.

Couture. Spring–Summer 1989.
Inspired by the *Nike* of Samothraces,
a draped evening gown
with embroidered insets of garlands
of small silver leaves and flowers.
Rome, Accademia Valentino.
Photo Daniel Jouanneau.

Couture. Fall–Winter 1986–87.
Red silk crêpe dress in neoclassical style.
Photo Noelle Hoeppe

Couture. Fall–Winter 1961–62.
White evening gown with train, edged in precious stones.
Photo Archivio Valentino.

Couture. Fall–Winter 1978–79.
Pleated pink lamé evening gown enriched by ruches.
Photo Archivio Valentino.

Couture. Spring–Summer 1972.
Flowing evening gown with lace inset.
Photo Archivio Valentino.

Couture. Fall–Winter 1974–75.
Salmon pink chiffon evening dress
with finely ruched bodice
and three flounces edged in marabou feathers.
Photo Archivio Valentino.

Page 290
Couture. Spring–Summer 1965.
Red crêpe evening dress
with full embroidered ostrich cape.
Photo Archivio Valentino.

Boutique. Fall–Winter 1988–89.
Evening gown with flounced lace and tulle skirt.
Photo Stefano Massimo/*Grazia* © Mondadori Press.

Page 292
Boutique. Fall–Winter 1988–89.
Evening dress made up of a violet bodice
on a yellow-gold skirt with exquisite openwork embroidery.
Photo David Seidner.

Page 294
Boutique. Fall–Winter 1997–98.
Dress in gray shot silk with bead and crystal appliqués.
Courtesy *Vogue* © 1997 Condé Nast Publications Inc.

Page 295
Couture. Spring–Summer 1995.
Claudia Schiffer in a long dress with underskirt
and full gray coat with embroidered neck and sleeves.
Photo Michel Comte/Courtesy *Vogue*.
©1995 Edizioni Condé Nast S.p.A.

V
alentino's
world

“My private world is a simple world. Every day I thank heaven for the life that it has given me. I have a great appetite for splendor, but at the same time very simple tastes. Nothing for me is better than a plate of thin pasta, *pennette* with tomato and basil sauce. I could eat it morning, noon, and night, at teatime, lunch, and dinner; it is so satisfying. But also, nothing is more seductive for me than the sight of those sublime gardens in Italy. I will always remember a crumbling wall under a great cascade of white roses that I saw at Marella Agnelli’s home; I cherish my memories of the most incredible landscapes in Italy. When I am on a glacier deep inside of me I am filled with emotion: before these marvelous immensities, everything, trivialities, feelings take on their true perspective. And the man that I am then knows it.”

Page 297
Photo of the set for Luchino Visconti’s film *The Leopard.*
Photo Giambattista Poletto/Courtesy Titanus.

Page 299
Photo Galen Rowell/Peter Arnold Inc./Grazia Neri.

Valentino may love fashion and its fabrics, homes and their furnishings, but one thing is clear: above all, Valentino loves life. Whether he is planning a trip, entertaining his friends, hiring a cook (only the best will do), or hunting down the most incredible finds in every major metropolis, the great couturier is caught up in it all with the same enthusiasm, the same relish. He is thankful for all that life has to offer him. "When I am alone, which upon occasion does happen," says Valentino "my greatest joy is to go settle into my favorite corner for reading or for sketching." The idea could not have been expressed more simply. But when it comes to guessing which room of his many homes Valentino prefers, he is hesitant about favoring this or that element, this or that object. Rome is his headquarters. But, paradoxically, since he works so intensely, he has little opportunity to enjoy the handsome neoclassical villa in via Appia. Capri is his summer vacation spot where life is simple. In Gstaad he owns a chalet that lends itself to long winter evenings. In London he recreated the elegantly languid atmosphere of the Victorian gentry; while in New York where he spends about one month of the year, Valentino owns an apartment, very ur-

A few interior and exterior views
of Valentino's
home in Rome.
Photos 1, 3, 5, Fritz von der Schulenburg. Photo 2, David Lees/*People*/Grazia Neri. Photo 4, Karen Radkai/Archivio Valentino. Photo 6, François Halard/Visual Team.

Page 301
Interior view of Valentino's home in Rome,
with painting by Fernando Botero.
Photo Fritz von der Schulenburg.

bane, with heavy red velvet draperies. But it is perhaps on his boat where he is able to forget the responsibilities linked to his ever-growing business. "The sea is the ultimate in protection. I leave everything behind me!"

When Valentino was just starting out in Paris, he lived in two *chambres de bonne.* He bought furniture by Boulle for a song at the *Marché aux Puces,* added some curtains and a few couches in *toile de Jouy.* It was not much, but it was charming. Success brought with it his first purchases: a seventeenth-century polychrome commode made in Rome, then an eighteenth-century *encoignure* and two still lifes that the *couturier* still has. The collecting mania has taken hold of him, and it will never let him go. Wherever he is, on the eve of a fashion show or between two fittings, the man (who is always pressed for time) slips away at the end to go in pursuit of the rare object, the handsome piece of furniture.

Rome, Palazzo Mignanelli. The office of Giancarlo Giammetti, president and managing director of the Valentino group. Photo François Halard/Visual Team.

Despite the diversity and the abundance of his homes, his interiors could not be less formal, less affected; they are a continual source of delight to the eye. "When I conceive an interior the first thing I think about is how many people I will be able to seat.

Discomfort along with pretention are the two worst things that can happen to a home."

Valentino has a passion for the most beautiful homes and the objects to fill them. It would therefore be unfair not to point out the sympathetic chord that this lively interest strikes in his partner, Giancarlo Giammetti. In both of their homes, as in their respective activities, their aesthetic is complementary: the atmosphere that surrounds the *couturier* evokes the Proustian charm of *temps perdus* from *The Leopard* of Lampedusa to Oscar Wilde's Belgravia. The businessman's setting is more contemporary: geared for action, it takes it inspiration from the Viennese Secession, the thirties, modern art. But they have the same unbridled passion for luxury and the same generosity. It is this curiosity that makes them alert to the slightest creative glimmer from wherever it comes.

Rome, Palazzo Mignanelli. Valentino's office. Photo François Halard/Visual Team.

Though Valentino loves to see his surroundings evolve and leads a cosmopolitan life, he would view it badly to constantly renew his interiors: "A clear personality flaw." In all the sense of the term, he is a creative. He wants his homes to conserve their integrity, to mature, to acquire a patina and slowly evolve.

It is the *couturier's* business to have this wisdom: "When I was a young designer, I made collections that incorporated two hundred thousand ideas where just thirty would have

PERIOD PATTERNS
COLEFAX & FOWLER

been enough. With time I learned to make real clothing for real women whose needs are real too. With homes it is the same thing. One must bear in mind certain constants that can be repeated in any period. There are certain traditions, proportions, and colors that must be respected. For me, for example, fabrics are a very important point of departure, the best way to personalize an interior. Along with very beautiful objects. The object has a magical effect on me. Later, one must learn to eliminate. Little by little one learns to distinguish that subtle line between too much and not enough that is called equilibrium. In fashion or in decor, it is the same thing: simplicity must never be redolent of poverty. One may even overdo, but only if it is done with great flair. To know how to exaggerate in moderation will always be the most difficult thing."

François Baudot

London, a few views of the interior of Valentino's home.
Photos Fritz von der Schulenburg.

Page 306
View of the Tuscan countryside.
Photo Marella Agnelli.

Page 307
Boutique. Fall–Winter 1992–93.
Sophia Loren dressed by Valentino.
Photo Michel Comte/
Courtesy *Vogue* © 1992
Edizioni Condé Nast S.p.A.

n our time fashion has definitely vanquished Marxism as the opiate of the masses. But Valentino's work is an exception. Although he has made his pact with the world as it is—with his licensed products, ready-to-wear, and so forth—his sensibility belongs to the happy few.

I use that expression with an accent on "happy". A Valentino collection at its best is an explosion of joy, a celebration not just of the glitter of wealth but of the sensual delights of life at the top. Of pleasure—like the joy of two lovers who hop into bed believing they own the world—ah yes, there's a lot of healthy sexiness in Valentino's style.

We all know that in real life rich people are not always happy and that Valentino himself may not be short of hang ups despite his success, but here's another important thing you have to recognize in his work: Valentino is a straightforward idealist.

This ideal, this Gatsby-like fascination with rarified, elegant bonheur may have its moral detractors. I happen to think a little of it is necessary to civilization, and I'm happy that in the case of Valentino it's in good hands. I used the word *straightforward.* I mean he doesn't deform his ideal because he's ashamed in our times to come right out with it. His fashion isn't ironic, it isn't off the wall, it isn't a cerebral diversion or worst of all, a publicity farce in the form of a tiresome intellectual joke. He doesn't make "avant-garde statements" to impress the multitudes.

Sometimes Valentino gets carried away with his enthusiasm and we get excess. But it's always innocent excess with a note of joy.

The distinctions between art and commerce or art and applied art have been blurred in our time. Without judging this historical change, I'd like to make reference to art in defining Valentino's work. You could say he is conceptually naïve and technically a master. Naive in the sense that his beliefs are untempered infatuations. He intends only one level of meaning. A master? You can count on your fingers the people in this world who have his technique. *Couturier* is a muchabused word nowadays, but this man is a true *couturier.*

I don't think Valentino—though he is known to eat off vermeil tableware—is really that much of a snob. As with Balenciaga, his style has a note of well-targeted emulation—the fascination of a talented person born poor but with an affinity for the taste of the most refined. His style does not arise from the self-adulation of a rock star.

He hasn't learned elegance at a remove, from magazines and the latest movies. His clients have refined him. However that kind of inspiring clientele is getting harder and harder to find.

Nonetheless, Valentino moves ahead with his times and he wins his case on the runways season after season, because after all is said, his creations are beautiful things. And a work of beauty stands firm as a work of beauty, no matter which way the wind is blowing.

Gerry Dryansky

Chronology

by Bonizza Giordani Aragno

1932

Born in Voghera, northern Italy. Grows into a calm, thoughtful child, uninterested in noisy games and fights. Takes refuge in a world of his own, where he makes drawings inspired by the paper patterns, silhouettes, and mannequins found in the millinery store owned by one of his aunts.

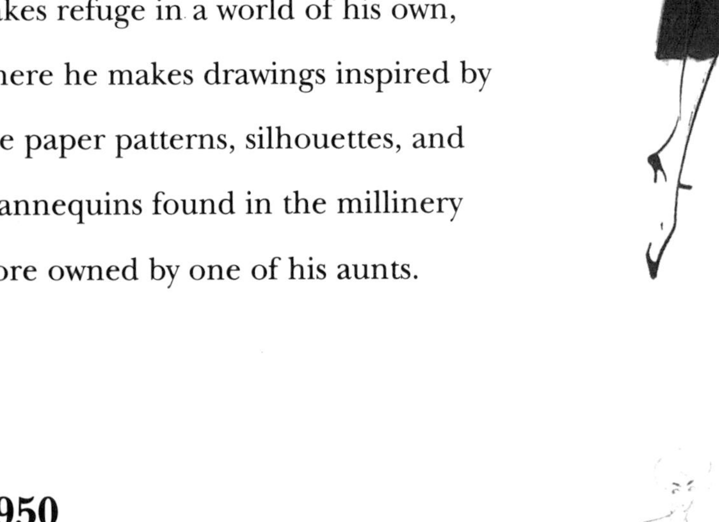

1950

Arrives in Milan, where he learns French and studies fashion design at the Via Santa Marta school. Moves to Paris, where he apprentices with Jean Dessès and Guy Laroche.

1959

Opens his first atelier in Rome.

1960

Meets Giancarlo Giammetti, an architecture student in Rome, who joins the house and eventually becomes its managing director.
Moves workshop to Via Gregoriana 54.
Elizabeth Taylor, in Rome filming *Cleopatra,* orders a white dress for the première of *Spartacus.*
Inaugurates a fashion line closely based on Couture.

1961

Spring–Summer collection characterized by romantic lines of evening gowns in gauze and tulle, similar to crinolines, trimmed with roses and wisteria blossoms.
Valentino's gowns photographed on the set of Federico Fellini's *8 1/2.*
Designs a black chiffon evening gown for Monica Vitti in the powder-compact scene in Michelangelo Antonioni's *La Notte.*
Shows twelve white satin dresses with wide jackets in a Jackie Kennedy style at the 1961 Fall–Winter collection at the Palazzo Barberini. "The look that inspires him is personal, intimate, captivating and sensual," writes *WWD.*

1962

Fall–Winter collection shown in Florence on July 19th, in an Haute Couture showcase at the Pitti Palace. Organizer, legendary Marchese Giorgini, gives him the last time slot of the last day. Incredible, surprising success. Foreign buyers, having heard of the designer, stay for the show. "There were buyers placing orders backstage at the end of the show—something that had not happened at any other show," reports Louise Hickman of the Associated Press.
Rome described as the new Hollywood.
Designs dresses for the big stars, from

Elizabeth Taylor to Rita Hayworth and Alida Valli. At Venice Film Festival, Valli, in a pink gown by Valentino, is singled out as the most elegant woman there. Luchino Visconti's *The Leopard* comes out. The film captures Valentino's imagination and influences the conception and style of his ballgowns.

1963

Fall–Winter collection: high waists, padded shoulders with sleeves fitted seven inches (18 cm) below them, as in Renaissance gowns, and crocodile hats. The line is revolutionary, and the reaction is violent.

"I rather liked it, but most of the professionals shook their heads, as if the innovation were too dramatic," Dino Buzzati observes in the *Corriere della Sera* of July 17th. "There were no interruptions, nobody murmured, 'But one cannot travel in the subway like that'; rather, it was as if all the subways had disappeared from the face of the earth and immense Cadillacs respectfully awaited the ladies in their Valentinos, solemn as Infantas of Spain," Irene Brin continues in *Giornale d'Italia* the same day. "As Valentino's first models appeared on the runway, Hamlet's dilemma presented itself: to accept or not to accept these new shoulders, with their fifteenth-century sleeves?" Maria Pezzi writes in the *Giorno.*

1964

Spring–Summer collection rich in ideas that will become the leitmotiv of a style: Empire line, pastel colors, the play of black and white, zoo fantasies.

March—American *Vogue* publishes a Valentino design for the first time: a black dress with a zebra-striped sequined jacket, worn by Countess Consuelo Crespi and photographed by Leombruno/Bodi. Valentino's consecration in the American press. July—at the Florence collections, place of honor reserved for Valentino. "Valentino's collection was indisputably Number One. Yesterday's show at the Pitti Palace carried the young designer, who is as handsome as he is 'sheikh,' to the top of the fashion world. He foresaw the return of the sleeve and made it the focal point of his line," Patricia Peterson reports the next day in the *New York Times.* Meets Jackie Kennedy for the first time, and designs a wardrobe for the former first lady, who is coming out of mourning for the President.

"For the second time in history women are sighing for a young man named Valentino. This time he's not an actor—a matinee idol—but an Italian designer who lives in Rome," Eugenia Sheppard writes in the *Houston Post.*

1965

Spring–Summer collection: tunics given definition by a thin belt and worn with

short, buttonless jackets. Distinctive fabrics, including ribbon lace and harem pajamas in Art Nouveau prints. "His evening pajamas, sometimes with a jacket, sometimes with draping, drew cries of enthusiasm from a very attentive packed house. I mean that, for once, all the buyers were there, all the international editors, all the young princesses and all the refined countesses, and the phantoms of Paul Poiret and Lucien Lelong," Irene Brin writes in the *Giornale d'Italia.*
"Valentino is making news in the world of fashion. Four years ago he was an unknown. Today he has his own house, and it's one of the most important in Rome. Last year he added Jackie Kennedy and Audrey Hepburn to his list of clients—a list that by now seems infinite," Patricia Peterson observes in the *New York Times.*
Fall–Winter collection: black and white. Inspired by op art and in particular by the "Responsive Eye" show at the Museum of Modern Art in New York.
"Valentino is a master at putting a simple white belt on a little black dress—of the type that all women have—and making it stand out," writes Irene Brin.
In the French magazine *Marie-Claire* several pages devoted to "the wild style of Virna Lisi," and a "new Italian designer with the romantic name of Valentino."
Designs a collection in leather for Leathermode, in New York.
Opens a branch in Milan on Via Sant'Andrea.

1966

Deserts Florence and presents Spring–Summer collection at his own showroom in Rome. Marks the return of the atelier as the sanctuary of fashion. Fashion inspired by pop art. Interprets it in a series of animal prints, in giraffe and black-and-white zebra patterns, and checks, stripes, and polka dots.
Princess Paola de Lièges, Jacqueline Kennedy, and Jacqueline de Ribes come to Rome to see Valentino.
May—article published in *Life* on Valentino, with a photograph of Princess Luciana Pignatelli in a red crêpe dress.
Fall–Winter collection characterized by loose coats, bias cuts, broader shoulders, bright colors, pants, a non-geometric and feminine line. Dyed furs introduced: pink and purple mink presented.
"Valentino plays the sweetest music in Rome. The first movement of the symphony of Italian Haute Couture was Valentino's fortissimo. The restless public, which had been waiting for an hour, was finally pacified when the reversible orange and mustard cape appeared, eliciting the first burst of applause," *WWD* reports the day after the show.

Valentino's clients include the most prestigious names. "The biggest buyer was Lord & Taylor with five coats, one dress and an evening pajama outfit; Bonwit Teller chose three coats; Saks two; Alexander's a coat and four evening dresses; Hess Bros. a coat and pants, a purple fox jacket, and a striped wool evening coat; I. Magnin chose three copies of the double wool gabardine pant suit in a leopard print; Montgomery Ward two suits for daytime; Evelyn Byrnes a coat-dress; Jerry Silverman a coat and a dress; Zelinka two coats; Hannah Troy an evening dress and two shawls, and Ohrbach's a coat. Even Ebony went for Valentino, going with the daywear, the after-ski, and the formal wear," *WWD* explains.

"Valentino raises the tone of Haute Couture in Rome. All the nonsense about how Haute Couture was being replaced by Prêt-à-porter went out the window after his astonishing opening show. Barely thirty, the young designer is already a master of refinement, a superb color artist, and a perfectionist whose design technique, which aims at simplified elegance and femininity, sparkles with new ideas and romantic atmosphere," observes Fay Hammond in the *Los Angeles Times.*

Designs his first lingerie collection. Creates Marella Agnelli's costume for the black-and-white ball given by Truman Capote at the Plaza Hotel in New York in December.

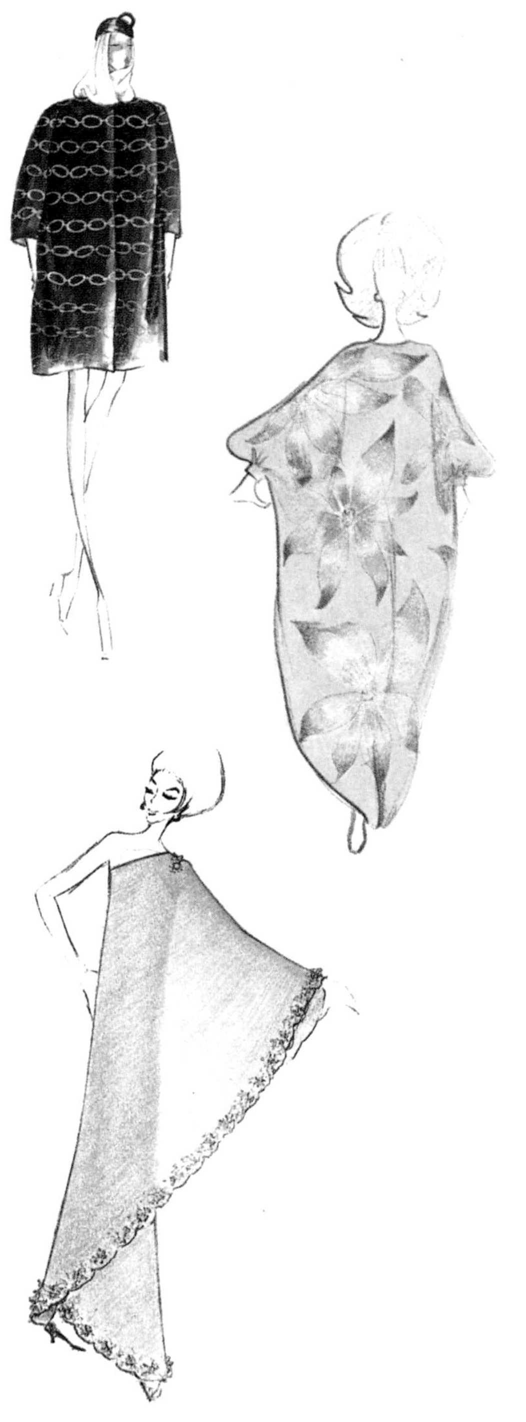

1967

Spring–Summer collection: caftan dresses, tarbooshes, and cowls, in chain prints; a clean style in which white and brown predominate. The logo "V" appears as a decorative element in the dresses. "He is an innovator, an extraordinary designer, an artist," declares Marian Christy, in the *Boston Globe.* "Valentino has climbed to the peak of success during the last year, because of the colors and the materials he uses, but above all because he is a volcano of new ideas, which, good or bad, are entirely his own," adds Gloria Emerson, in the *New York Times.* "His clients now include Gloria Guinness, Babe Paley, Ethel Scull, Annette Reed, Jayne Wrightsman, Christina Ford," *WWD* reports. February 9th—receives the Neiman Marcus Award in Dallas; four days later receives the Martha Award in Palm Beach. Story on Jacqueline Kennedy in Cambodia written in *Life.* In all the photos she is wearing Valentino.

"Valentino's wonderful clothes are a sensation on the streets of New York, Paris, Rome, London. But in Cambodia? Fashion demonstrates that Jackie's elegance has succeeded in softening the granite of Communist hearts. And no one can deny it," Marian Christy writes in the *Boston Globe*.

September—presents his collection in New York. "Valentino arrived in New York late Tuesday evening. And Wednesday morning women were already knocking at the door of his apartment in the St. Regis: Anne Ford Uzelli and her sister Charlotte Niarchos, Mrs. Wrightsman, Mrs. Kennedy, Mrs. Guinness, Kay Graham, Countess Jacqueline de Ribes," *WWD* observes. Designs raincoats for the Lawrence of London line, in New York, and uniforms for TWA flight attendants.

Shows his first Valentino Uomo collection in the winter of 1967.

"'V' for Valentino: covered with Vs from her ears to the tip of her shoes, this beautiful Roman wears a model by the most 'in' Italian designer of the moment, whose name, naturally, is Valentino," *Life* reports in November.

Starts designing accessories; handbags with the gold "V," produced by Coppola and Toppo, immediately become the must-have accessory.

A revolution in advertising: first *groupage* of a single designer introduced. Giancarlo Giammetti gives it to Gian Paolo Barbieri for Italian *Vogue*, a new magazine published by Condé Nast.

1968

Spring–Summer collection completely white: coats, dresses, striped sweaters, organza, chiffon, scarves draped around the neck, lace-embroidered stockings. "The Americans are mad for this Italian who, in a mere eight years, has become the king of fashion," *WWD* observes. And adds: "Valentino is rekindling the lights of Rome. He has another success. Once again the buyers ran out of superlatives as they left his salon."

"Valentino's striking collection: when Valentino opened the Rome shows people were so dazzled that they wanted to expand the shows into a 'fashion week.' The young designer, who is already the favorite of Jacqueline Kennedy and others whose names often appear in the gossip columns, has demonstrated that he has the artistic stature capable of changing the mood of the fashion world from evening to morning," E. Lambert writes in the *Oklahoma City*.

March—after the show, at Lord & Taylor in New York some 900 Valentino dresses, at prices ranging from $100 to $395, are sold.

Opens a boutique on Avenue Montaigne, in Paris.

Show at the St. Regis, in New York, attended by Princess Margaret.

Time Magazine runs article on Valentino: "Valentino the Victorious. At thirty-five, he can already count on an unsurpassable list of clients who come to his salon on Via Gregoriana 54. In the first rank is Jackie Kennedy, who rarely buys elsewhere. And, what's crucial, Valentino improves over time. At every new collection the editorialists of fashion decree that it is better than the one before. As *Vogue* reports, Valentino has become the idol of the new generation, the new symbol of modern luxury."

Fall–Winter collection based on brown and black. Full ballerina skirts, fitted tops. Boots and capes very much in evidence.

"Sometimes one comes out of a Broadway show humming the tunes. Valentino puts on that kind of show. One leaves with the desire to take away all his creations. What Valentino did for white last season he does this time for black," Eugenia Sheppard writes in the *International Herald Tribune.*

Look devotes seven pages to Valentino: "The new sheikh of chic: Valentino. Why do women love him? The answer is: Valentino is perfection. He has created a youthful, slender line, universally seductive, which appears simple but is based, according to his own words, on a 'complex structure—like architecture.' He is so attentive to details that every woman knows exactly what accessories to wear."

October—designs dress for Jacqueline Kennedy's marriage to Aristotle Onassis. Sixty orders arrive from around the world for identical models.

In Capri receives the first Tiberio d'Oro award.

At the Grande Ballo Patino in Estoril, Portugal, fifty women wearing Valentino.

November—shows designs at the Savoy in London, for the benefit of the Invalid Children's Aid Association, under patronage of Princess Margaret.

1969

Spring–Summer: a gypsy collection, featuring full, flounced skirts, coral jewelry, and fringed ponchos; for the first time the show has a musical accompaniment in the background, marking the start of the fashion show as theater.

"Was it a collection worthy of Valentino? Yes, of course. But we did not really see it: the 'choreography' has the lion's share, and all that skipping about, coming and going, up and down, back and forth, completely bewildered me. A piece-by-piece review will follow (as I will see it again)," Irene Brin comments in the *Corriere di Informazione.*

Stern devotes March cover and six-page spread to Valentino's gypsy collection.

Boutique line inaugurated. Produced by Mendès, a French company.

Fall–Winter dresses are part of an extremely luxurious collection: overcoats, bathrobes, crocodile prints, toga-style evening gowns, sable-trimmed floor-length capes—all in beige tones. Also fringed shawls, and pants.

"Many are called (in this case the self-invited) to the banquet of Haute Couture, but the chosen, who have something to say and say it with authority, are very few. Among these is Valentino, who has presented one of his most beautiful collections. Rarely does one see a show that opens as the one yesterday evening did, with 15 or 20 models, rigorously chosen, in particular shades of beige, champagne, sand, butter, camel, and leather," Maria Pezzi writes the next day in the *Giorno*. "Valentino has created a collection that drew applause from sweaty hands and roars of admiration from a public that was suffocating in the heat of the evening," Ernestine Carter writes in the *Sunday Times*. "The verdict: this is one of Valentino's best collections from every point of view—line, fabrics, and ideas. Once again the fans cry 'Bravo,'" June Weir reports in *WWD*.

1970

Spring–Summer: straight, hard-edged line, but with new softness and new length. Under midi coats the skirts are short. "The midi explodes with Valentino," *WWD* says in its headline. "The demand for seats at the new Valentino collection was so great that the hero of Italian fashion had to slice a piece off the runway to make room for thirty more people. These are the problems one must face when one is called Valentino. But no one in the world of fashion could bear to remain outside a show like his, which left all the others in the dust," Gloria Emerson writes in the *New York Times*.

Lowers hemlines. "There is no doubt that Valentino's new look has jolted the buyers. Whether or not they liked the midi length, they all loved what Valentino did with it. And no one could have done better" writes *WWD*.

"Luxurious, diverting, magnificent dresses in enchanting colors. . . . Valentino demonstrates all his mastery in some of the most beautiful coats that have ever been seen," American *Vogue* reports. "Valentino creates a new length for the seventies," *Harper's Bazaar* America writes.

April—Valentino boutique opens in Rome.

Fall–Winter collection: midi length continues, in designs inspired by Tartar culture, with important new proportions.

"Valentino is the ringmaster of the circus of fashion. He has produced the greatest show on Italian earth," *WWD* comments.

October—Valentino boutique opens on Madison Avenue in New York, as well as boutiques in the I. Magnin stores in San Francisco and Los Angeles,

Nan Duskin in Philadelphia, Kaufman's in Pittsburgh, and Neusteter's in Denver.

1971

Spring–Summer collection inspired by the thirties, and by Hollywood stars from Betty Grable to Marilyn Monroe. Reintroduces hot pants, for day and evening. "He has succeeded in a nearly impossible undertaking. He has captured, almost in its entirety, the spirit of the thirties and has made it compatible with the present," Bernadine Morris observes in the *New York Times.*

Fall–Winter collection: nearly all in black and white, in homage to Garbo in *Bonnie and Clyde.*

November—Valentino boutiques open in Geneva and Lausanne.

December—Giovanni Leone becomes the sixth President of the Republic of Italy. From now on Vittoria Leone, wearing Valentino, will export Italian elegance all over the world.

In New York Andy Warhol draws Valentino.

1972

Spring–Summer collection: a romantic collection, which introduces the floral look, recalling *Death in Venice.*

"The person responsible for this remembrance, Luchino Visconti, who is thinking of Ludwig of Bavaria and studies Marcel Proust, surrounded by characters from the film *The Damned,* Marisa Berenson and Helmut Berger, does not miss a detail," Pia Soli explains in *Tempo.*

"It was a triumphant show. The audience, which included many movie stars, did not stop applauding and shouting 'Bravo.' Valentino himself appeared overcome by emotion as he walked down the runway greeting his fans. The look of the barricades is over, now there is only luxury and femininity," *WWD* reports. "Naturally, many people would like to see him fall on his face, those who cannot forgive him for being the only reason that the Roman shows keep going. Everyone comes to Rome to see Valentino, and, once here, people pay a quick visit to other shows. And this time Valentino did not make a single false step. An air of authority emanates from the whole show, from the moment when three models in white coats with batwing sleeves enter to the disappearance of three evening gowns worthy of a graduation party at Yale in 1952. It is the type of collection that changes the look of fashion," Bernadine Morris writes in the *New York Times.*

March—Valentino Uomo and Valentino Più boutiques launched in Via Condotti. Latter devoted to household furnishings: Valentino's interests broaden into other areas, not strictly limited to clothing.

Elizabeth Taylor and Audrey Hepburn wear Valentino to the ball of the century, organized in January by the Baron and Baroness Rothschild in their castle of Ferrières for the centenary of the birth of Marcel Proust.

"Audrey was all simplicity and charm, like a young girl at a picnic," Cecil Beaton recalls.

Anjelica Huston appears as a special model for the Spring–Summer ad campaign, produced by the photographer Gian Paolo Barbieri.

Fall–Winter collection: pants abolished; boxy jackets, fox trim, Chinese prints. A lot of lamé and chiffon, and the sweater look.

1973

Spring–Summer collection inspired by the art of Gustav Klimt.

"Valentino presents a garden party. His new collection has more ruffles, ribbon rosettes, intarsias, and romantic pastel colors than Cecil Beaton's famous scene of Ascot in *My Fair Lady*," Eugenia Sheppard comments in the *New York Post*.

"If Valentino didn't exist—this is one of the stories that circulate widely among people in the fashion industry—the buyers and journalists of American fashion would have had to invent him to have an excuse for going to Rome twice a year," Marylou Luther says jokingly in the *Los Angeles Times*.

Vittoria Leone chooses her wardrobe from Valentino for state visits to the United States and France. "The wardrobe of the president's wife is splendid. This is why we should be proud of it: it is the best expression of what we, in Italy, have been able to create in the area of fashion, an art that until twenty years ago was the exclusive prerogative of France," Pia Soli observes in *Tempo*.

Fall–Winter collection inspired by Léon Bakst's designs for ballets.

The great protagonist of the Boutique line is the sweater. "The sweater has the starring role. Valentino begins and ends his new fall collection with the sweater, but it's not an ordinary sweater, and for the hour that the show lasts it meets with more adventures than the heroine of a soap opera," Eugenia Sheppard says in the *New York Post*.

"Valentino is terrific. He has designed a deluxe collection for the woman of luxury. His Boutique line, very close to the Haute Couture, is simply fantastic. This is the true Valentino. It is an intellectual collection in all the right colors," writes *WWD*.

"All the roads of fashion lead to Valentino in Rome," Bernadine Morris concludes in the *New York Times*.

1974

Spring–Summer collection recalls the atmosphere of films like *The Great Gatsby* and *The Garden of the Finzi-Contini*: pleated skirts, tennis sweaters, a profusion of linen and of white.

"Feminine, relaxed, simple, sexy: in these words Valentino describes the woman for whom he has designed this season. They serve also to describe the collection itself," Joan Buck sums up in *WWD.* "The new atmosphere at Valentino's in Rome is more delicate: fine as the finest lingerie, especially a series of soft evening gowns cut on the bias," American *Vogue* observes. "Valentino's collection has 'the most of the most.' It is the most luxurious and costly production ever to appear on a runway in recent years. It is the most youthful and seductive interpretation seen up to now of the long skirt, and it creates a new record for furs, feathers, and beads," Eugenia Sheppard writes in the *International Herald Tribune.* "The first to arrive was Princess Grace of Monaco, then her daughter Caroline, with the expression that a charming girl of sixteen has when she is always accompanied by a strict bodyguard. She said she had come to Rome to have fun, which that day included the Valentino show," *WWD* reports.

September—Valentino boutique opens in London, in Sloane Street. Opening followed by a fashion show and a gala at the Savoy, attended by Princess Margaret.

Valentino boutique opens at Bloomingdale's in New York.

1975

Slim suits, narrow jackets over pleated skirts, shoulders accentuated by new shoulder pads. "The king of Italian fashion, Valentino, sheathes his woman in skirts so tight that every curve is visible and they have to have pleats to enable the legs to move," *Newsweek* writes.

April—receives the Mode Woche prize in Munich.

Shows the Fall–Winter Boutique line in Paris, at the Hôtel George V, for the first time. Designs inspired by Asian styles and cultures.

Couture shows will remain in Rome. "Valentino created waves of admiration at his first show in Paris. He arrived, they saw him, and were conquered by him," Alison Lerrick of the Associated Press writes. "Milan is indisputably No.1 as the capital of Italian Prêt-à-porter. What is in dispute, however, is that the No. 1 Italian designer shunned Milan for Paris to show his new Boutique collection," *WWD* writes. "Valentino has found a response so seductive and so bewitching in its proportions that, in my opinion, women will not wait for fall to appropriate this new look," Prudence Glynn writes in the *New York Times.*

May—the great Valentino boutique opens on 19, Avenue Montaigne in Paris. Largest point of sale of any of the fifty that have opened so far (1500 square feet). Another boutique, on the Faubourg Saint-Honoré, opens a month later.

September—Valentino boutique opens

on Fifth Avenue in New York. "For the opening of the Valentino boutique on Fifth Avenue, more than a thousand guests (who had to be protected by police barricades from the throng of passersby) poured into the bottle-shaped store, which is decorated in beige and with mirrors, and many were driven out like champagne corks," the *Daily News* reports the next day.

1976

Spring–Summer collection: a wealth of ethnic motifs drawn from the Arab world. Wide harem pants with chiffon tops, kaffiyehs, long patchwork tunics over wide-legged pants.

"Valentino, like Saint-Laurent and Madame Grès, is one of the few creators of fashion who still insist on a clear difference between Couture and Prêt-à-porter. 'One who was born in Couture,' Valentino says, 'cannot abandon it,'" writes *WWD*. "At the close of the collections, Valentino once again managed to go against the current and at the same time emphasize the costume trend of the moment," Lucia Sollazzo observes in the *Stampa*.

Fall–Winter Boutique collection in Paris. "The reason Valentino's clothes are fresher and more attractive than everything else that was shown in Paris in the same price range is, obviously, that he has devoted more time to creating them," Marylou Luther explains in the *Los Angeles Times*.

Big Valentino boutique opens in Tokyo in the Hotel New Otani.

June—presents a show at the Hotel Pierre in New York to benefit the Special Olympics for Retarded Children, a charity sponsored by the Kennedy family. "Kennedy plus Valentino equals magic," Bernadine Morris writes in the *New York Times*.

Fall–Winter: a deluxe sportswear collection. Knickers worn over lizard boots; pullovers and capes; hoods that become part of the pullover.

"It's as if Valentino, like a writer who decides after the passage of time to rewrite one of his novels, had closely examined his style, and eliminated every self-indulgence and every excessive adjective, and here and there added new, vigorous touches," Italian *Vogue* comments.

1977

Spring–Summer Boutique: an all-white collection, inspired by Brazil and especially by Bahia.

"With Valentino imagination conquers all. His spectacular show, with a setting worthy of a Broadway musical, put everyone in a good mood. The show began with the lights trained on a Bahia dancer, and as he danced a solo, the stage, hidden behind him, rose, bringing forward thirty models dressed in white. The impact of this collection was immediate, and caused great excitement among the buyers," *WWD* reports.

"It was the most captivating show opening ever seen in Paris. The models, male and female, appeared all together on the stage, like an orchestra, swaying and smiling to the sounds of a Latin-American beat. They were all in white: off-the-shoulder blouses, flounced skirts and ruffled petticoats, aprons and similar elements. The idea came from Brazil, but the effect was that of a group of bright young people such as are found everywhere," Bernadine Morris writes in the *Times.*

Spring–Summer Couture: again, a lot of white but more romanticism and more luxury, especially in the ballgowns, inspired by Vienna and the Central European tradition.

"V as in victory and in Valentino. Once there was the C: it stood for Coco Chanel. Now the V, V as in victory: and it means Valentino. He is one of the two great men of fashion: the other would be Yves Saint-Laurent. Gloria Guinness, who is considered the most elegant woman in the world, has said: 'You see, I don't wear his clothes, I love them,' and it is a compelling declaration," Enzo Biagi writes in the pages of the *Corriere della Sera.*

Fall–Winter Couture: line based on the

blouson. Full-skirted coats.

Fall–Winter Boutique: collection inspired by Visconti's *Ludwig*, illustrated magnificently in the photographs of Deborah Turbeville.

"He is the Mr. Chic of Italian Haute Couture," *WWD* decrees.

September—three Valentino boutiques open in New York at Bonwit Teller: Couture, Uomo, and Valentino Più.

New York celebrates Valentino for four days.

1978

Spring–Summer Boutique: cool and fresh, with pastel colors and romantic details in a garden-party atmosphere.

Spring–Summer Couture: linear, pure, simple, unfitted collection. A lot of linen, and a softness in the shoulders.

"Valentino's slim line had a great success in Rome. He is still the indisputable sovereign of Italian fashion. His dresses, with such clean lines, in fabrics that run from linen to georgette, made the show a success," *WWD* comments.

Fall–Winter Couture: the "*melone*" style is introduced, which is narrower at the bottom.

Fall–Winter Boutique line: designs a collection inspired by the past with bathrobes over gold pants and bathing suit lines. The advertising photographs are by Horst.

"Valentino's lovely collection marched through a red lacquer revolving door while a man played jazz on a player piano. He uses luxurious fabrics for softly enveloping coats of great beauty," *WWD* reports.

October—introduction of the perfume Valentino, at the Théâtre des Champs-Elysées, in Paris. "A night like this couldn't happen anywhere in the world but Paris," says Lauren Bacall, interviewed by *WWD*.

"Valentino and Giancarlo Giammetti did things on the grand scale: high fashion, high creativity, and great hopes for celebrating the birth of the perfume Valentino in France. The fragrance's début took place at the Théâtre des Champs Elysées, with the music of Tchaikovsky, Roland Petit's ballet, and the interpretation of Mikhail Baryshnikov, who performed the *Queen of Spades* for the first time. After the show, there was a gala dinner for 260 people at Maxim's and a gigantic buffet at Le Palace," *WWD* reports.

1979

Spring–Summer Boutique: a colorful, carefree collection. The show, at the Cirque d'Hiver in Paris, had a circus atmosphere.

"Valentino has created one of the most successful, handsome, and easy-to-wear collections of his already astounding career. His message for 1979 is a 'total woman' woman," Marylou Luther writes in the *Los Angeles Times.*

"With Andy Warhol taking photographs and Baron Guy de Rothschild taking notes, Valentino doesn't seem to have any problem in being accepted. His collection is refined, with a great freshness of colors and effects. He has added a new dimension to Paris fashion, which at times is too serious," reports Hebe Dorsey in the *International Herald Tribune.*

Spring–Summer Couture: geometric, boxy collection.

"The most famous Italian designer in the world astonishes us every time with the richness of his collections.
But if it is Haute Couture, the richness is appropriate. He invents unstintingly, with variations on the theme,
the materials, the details, the execution, always satisfying a public of women swooning for Valentino,"
Adriana Mulassano comments in the *Corriere della Sera.*

"But then there is the restraint,
the taste, the skill that Valentino has acquired, through which he can evoke
a hundred ideas from the past without ever seeming retro: it would be a pity
if Valentino abandons Rome as he has already abandoned the Camera della Moda," Maria Pezzi observes in the *Giorno.*

"Italian Haute Couture is grateful.
Valentino will remain. The good news is

that Valentino has decided not to move his operations to Paris, and has thus saved Italian Haute Couture from collapse," Hebe Dorsey writes in the *International Herald Tribune.*

May—big party organized by Steve Rubell in New York for Valentino's birthday, transforming his Studio 54 into a circus. Also at Studio 54, Valentino's jeans collection introduced. Advertising photographs taken by an unknown young photographer, Bruce Weber.

Fall–Winter Couture: fall and winter collection, "Shades," has Dada and surrealist echoes and features trompe-l'œil games.

The house of Valentino leaves Mendès and joins the GFT group for the production of its Boutique lines.

1980

Spring–Summer Boutique: intarsias, playing with transparency, organza and linen, gray and white.

"Valentino, our designer-designer (that is, double-barrelled designer) was eagerly engulfed—at the end of the runway—by shouts of applause and the embraces of his yellow, white, and black models, all with extremely long legs," Nanda Calandri writes in the *Messaggero.*

Spring–Summer Couture: long-waisted tutus, lavish embroidery, artisanal workmanship. Transparent black blouses with white collars.

"The pope of fashion has put out his summer manifesto. Delicious short flared skirts, long close-fitting bodices, fluttering white collars, and marvelous black-sequined and white crêpe evening gowns. At the end of the show everyone was in ecstasy," *WWD* reports.

Fall–Winter: collection based on the elaboration of detail, culottes, and a new "new look" with fullness, tight-fitting jackets, tones of camel and brown, and a lot of black.

"Valentino is always Valentino. If it weren't for him, Haute Couture would be dying: his show alone still succeeds in bringing to Rome the leading players of international fashion," notes *Donna.*

1981

Spring–Summer Couture collection presents a spiral line for evening with a scoop on the runway: Brooke Shields (fifteen years old) appears as a special model for Valentino.

"As if the emotions of the show were not already intense, Valentino added a piquant touch, seating in the front row such personalities as Françoise Sagan, flown here from Paris, and Paloma Picasso, just arrived from New York. The two women spent their money well. The only international designer in Rome was extremely successful, with a collection that gloriously sums up his approach to great fashion: super clothes for superstars, luxury for the love of luxury and to hell with the expense!" Hebe Dorsey writes in the *International Herald Tribune.*

Introduces jodhpurs in the Boutique collection.

"Valentino's creations are always sexy, even when they are unbelievable, like over-the-knee jodhpurs worn with hats, lacy blouses, fringed scarfs, large fabric roses on collars, necklaces, earrings, and fabulous belts, and the background music is *The Age of Aquarius*, from the original soundtrack of *Hair.* The hippies would have died," Priscilla Tucker writes enthusiastically in the *Daily News.*

A February issue of *Time* devotes its cover, "The 80s Look," to Brooke Shields dressed by Valentino.

The Alfa Romeo 1200 comes out, baptized "Alfa Sud by Valentino," in a metallic bronze with a black roof.

Fall–Winter line: long, capacious coats, in Scottish plaids. Slim suits underneath; sexy and dramatic evening wear.

"Valentino's capacity to reinvent himself every season is incredible—but what am I saying? I mean every three months, because between the two big Couture collections are the two Prêt-à-porter collections, the Cruise collection, Miss V, and then he has to oversee all the licenses that have made him the busiest and most widely distributed Italian designer in the world," Pia Soli claims

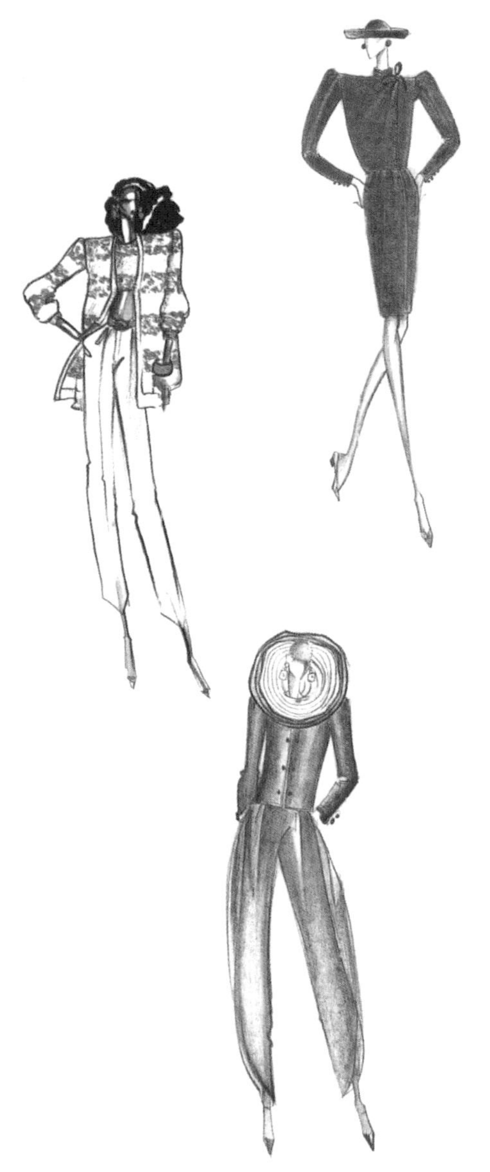

in *Tempo.*

In Rome the Istituto Nazionale per la Grafica presents the show "Haute Couture Design from 1930 to 1970," the first exhibition of Italian fashion design.

1982

Spring–Summer Boutique: Chinese-lantern-style bloomers, pouf skirts, a symphony of black and white.

"Valentino has an extraordinary ability to give a luxurious treatment to difficult lines: all those shorts, bloomers, and pants that seem more suitable to a public of penniless youths. He succeeds with a rounded cut that makes them billow like boxing shorts," Hebe Dorsey eulogizes in the *International Herald Tribune.* "Despite his comparative sobriety, it may be that Valentino has inherited the mantle of Paul Poiret. Poiret's famous lampshade dress, which made history in the early part of the century, is at least the spiritual antecedent of the short lampshade pants that the Italian designer has shown for wearing at home," Bernadine Morris writes in the *New York Times.*

Spring–Summer Couture: straight line that swells at the bottom, giving an effect of balance. Long jackets. Other skirts resemble sarongs, still others have an angled cut.

"The skirts that made the faithful, who had come to Rome expressly to see this collection, jump up in their seats are the sarongs, which are taken up on one side to reveal a lot of leg, and the 'guillotine' skirts, cut on an angle and with an irregular hem," Pia Soli reports in *Tempo.*

"What Valentino wants Valentino gets. And he deserves it. In what was the best and only true show of Rome's fashion week, he triumphed with a Spring–Summer collection that is boldly 'haute,' like the world in which he and his clients travel," Hebe Dorsey writes in the *International Herald Tribune.*

"At Valentino's, the mystique of Couture is still all there, even if he expresses concern that 'he will not be able to keep it up much longer.' The indispensable seamstresses and atelier workers have become an endangered species in Rome, and Valentino predicts that Couture as he knows it will probably last only a few more years. When his current workers retire, there will no longer be young ones to replace them," Patrick McCarthy reports in *WWD.*

On Oscar night Jane Fonda, wearing Valentino, accepts the Academy Award for her father, Henry Fonda, who is gravely ill.

October—Franco Maria Ricci publishes the exquisite volume *Valentino,* with text by André Leon Talley: it is an homage to the couturier's life, with drawings and photographs of his collections, which have been hallmarks of an era.

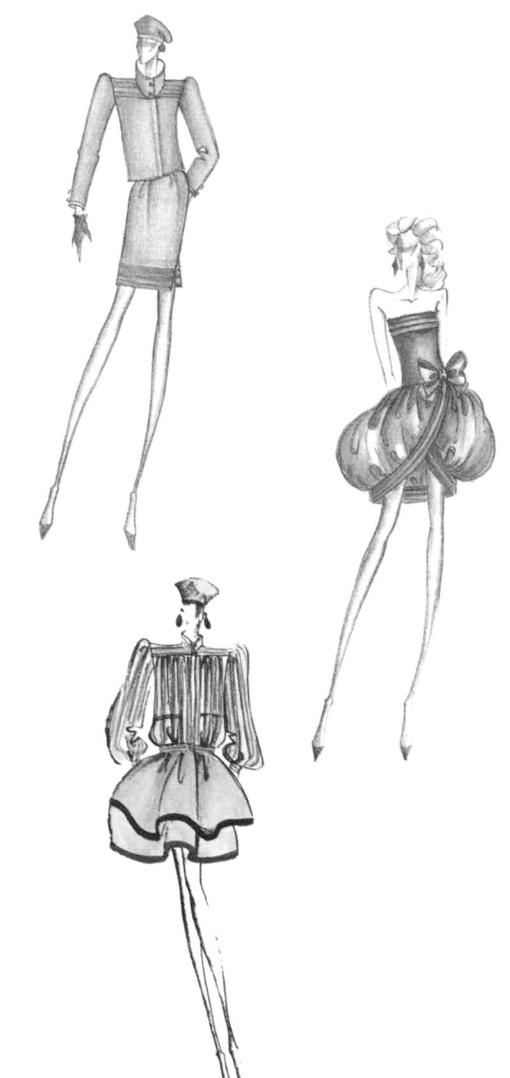

Fall–Winter Boutique: tight skirts, velvet bustiers. Everything is close-fitting, sexy. Python, leather, satin used together.

"For the first time, an Italian has won the hearts of Paris. The Parisians bestowed on him a triumphal ovation of a type normally reserved only for the chosen few who are members of their exclusive club. Valentino, the Latin lover of fashion, succeeded with a collection, created in Rome, that brought a contagious joy to the cloudy skies of the French capital. Valentino received praise that has been long overdue, but Paris is hard on foreign competition, and the Italian designers are frankly despised," Hebe Dorsey writes in the *International Herald Tribune.*

"Valentino, who for years has presented his Haute Couture collection only in Paris, is perhaps the first Italian to earn applause, and even ovations to the point of boredom, in this chauvinist country," Natalia Aspesi confirms in the *Repubblica.*

"The stroke of genius came, of course, from Valentino. A magic touch: in fashion this touch, which has the bold simplicity of the obvious, means the capacity to bring together various trends into something new that impresses by incorporating all of them," Lucia Sollazzo declares in the *Stampa.*

Fall–Winter Couture: an ultrasexy collection, with dresses that fit like a second skin, gored skirts, extreme décolletés. A lot of pink, and black-and-white. For day, reversible coats and skirts.

"Valentino, the master of Italian elegance, has revealed a new aspect of his artistic character, with a bold Fall–Winter collection that will infuse heat into the coldest months of the year," Daniela Petroff of the Associated Press writes.

"It is the greatest achievement of breathtaking chic. A few hours before, Giancarlo Giammetti had said: 'This is the most beautiful collection that Valentino has ever created,' and it may be true. The show was a stellar performance that united a new, more restrained elegance to innovative techniques and some of his famous decorative touches," *WWD* reports.

September—presents Fall–Winter collection at the invitation of Diana Vreeland at the Metropolitan Museum in New York. Vreeland declares: "Valentino's women can stand only in an art museum."

"A thousand people were invited to the illustrious American museum. Members of the New York City Ballet and American Ballet Theatre were on duty, surrounding masters such as Balanchine, Jerome Robbins, and Suzanne Farrell. Also present were Liza Minnelli, Raquel Welch and Richard Gere, Placido Domingo and Muhammad Ali, Brooke Shields and Diana Vreeland. Italian television broadcast it live by satellite," Furio Colombo reports in the *Stampa.*

1983

Spring–Summer Couture: a T line, emphasizing shoulders; straight sack dresses; black and white.

"He transforms an ordinary seam into a detail of pure Chic: the Chic of super Couture," writes *WWD.*

"Valentino's woman is proud and inaccessible, a cold 'sophisticated lady,' mysterious and off-putting. She can be tender or intransigent, capricious and sexy, but she inspires awe through the perfect aplomb with which she tempers every flirtation," writes Laura Laurenzi in the *Repubblica.* Receives the Seven Kings of Rome prize in the Campidoglio in Rome, with Sordi, Fellini, Andreotti, Gassman, Baglioni, and Falcao. Jessica Lange wins an Academy Award for *Tootsie* and accepts the Oscar in a sequined dress by Valentino in two tones of jade green.

Fall–Winter Boutique: collection dominated by broad, soft lines for day and shiny fabrics for evening. Full, calf-length skirts. "Valentino arrives and is immediately triumphant. The collection stands out as an ode to the most resounding successes of the season," Pia Soli writes in *Tempo.*

"The poor little rich girl doesn't exist for Valentino. His girls are rich but filled with joy. They travel a gilded highway from Acapulco to Gstaad, and spend their lives jumping from private jet to private yacht. The amazing thing about Valentino is that for years he has served us a solid diet based on pure luxury but has managed to keep it light and entertaining. His creativity is inexhaustible," Hebe Dorsey remarks in the *International Herald Tribune.*

"The French are fortunate to have Valentino. The retailers were enthusiastic about the collection, and praised both the day and the evening wear," *WWD* reports.

Fall–Winter Couture: shows at Piazza Mignanelli in front of a thousand people for the first time, opening with the uniforms he has designed for the Italian athletes who will participate in the Los Angeles Olympics.

Luxurious collection, featuring ankle-length skirts, and sequined tubes with jet fringe.

"For night? These are gowns for receiving an Oscar, for being received at Court, and for going to international balls," Paola Pisa observes in the *Messaggero.*

"It is elegance pushed to the limit," Valentino himself declares to *WWD.*

"Valentino interprets Rome. The collection he showed outside, in front of a thousand people in the Piazza di Spagna, was one of his most dynamic. But beyond the spectacle there was also important fashion news: the tunic, or rather what Valentino calls 'the little black dress,' short or long, in silk velvet or wool crêpe. It was the guiding principle of his new tapered look, enveloped in lamé and draped scarves," *WWD* reports.

November—takes part in Best Fives, the show organized in Tokyo by *WWD;* the other participants are Norma Kamali, Hanae Mori, Sonia Rykiel, Kansai Yamamoto.

Designs the costumes for Giuseppe Patroni Griffi's *Metti una sera a cena* at the Teatro Nuovo in Milan.

1984

Spring–Summer Boutique: long jackets, tight skirts. Everything is straight and slim. Cardigans over pleated skirts. Advertising photographs by Helmut Newton.

"An advocate for the beauty of the body, Valentino presented a silhouette that hugs the body, so close-fitting that it will be difficult for his clients to eat more than a lettuce leaf," Hebe Dorsey remarks in the *International Herald Tribune.*

"After the exhausting, exciting shows of the new French, Italian, Japanese, and English designers, after the surprises reserved by the grand old names who are always updating, to see Valentino at the Bois de Boulogne was a wonderful respite. Above all, the models were happy. Finally, they were not being asked to grime their faces and walk like sleepwalkers or madwomen, but to be beautiful, perfectly made up, and coiffed as God commands, and were able to advance along the runway as they like, swinging their hips with belly-dancer-like accents, their hands finally free to touch hips and shoulders allusively. The models were content: the press relaxed. Valentino put everything back in order," Natalia Aspesi writes in the *Repubblica*. "A great elegance joined with impeccable technique. A lovely end of the day," Janie Samet confirms in *Le Figaro*.

"Valentino dictates the new rules. When Valentino speaks, even if it's in Italian, everyone listens—including the French. At the end of his show at the Pavillon d'Armenonville, the spectators waved their arms, feeling stimulated, inspired, and professionally renewed. Valentino did not do things terribly different from the others, he only did them better," *WWD* reports.

Spring–Summer Couture: a triumph of evening gowns, with fishtail hems and in reptile and crocodile prints. Details, drapes, pleats, hourglass-shaped inserts and lines.

"In less masterly hands it could have been a disaster, but Valentino, the

wizard of the winds, transformed into pure magic his Haute Couture collection for spring and summer," *WWD* confirms. Valentino designs the wardrobe for Queen Sofia of Spain's visit to the Kremlin.

Fall–Winter Boutique combines sumptuous and sporty cardigans and twin sets in rich materials.

"The visual impact was dramatic, but all the clothes looked easy to wear. The designer from Rome has beaten the French at their own game: by making dresses that are sumptuous and sexy at the same time," Bernadine Morris writes in the *New York Times*. "They say that it was the most enthusiastically applauded show in Paris, which is ironic, because Valentino in effect is universal. His fashion house and his workshop are in Rome, but he always knows precisely what wealthy women everywhere in the world want to wear. In all probability, he has had the greatest success of the season," the journalist adds.

Rome—celebrates, in Piazza Mignanelli, along with his Haute Couture collection, his silver anniversary with fashion. On this occasion Valentino receives recognition from the Minister of Industry Renato Altissimo for his contribution to fashion and costume. At the Quirinale, where the couturier makes an offical visit, he is photographed with President Sandro Pertini for the cover of *Linea Italiana*.

Fall–Winter collection devoted to

woman as goddess and as seductress. "The fundamentals of the line, the ever-present femininity, the skill of the execution make these clothes masterpieces, works for a museum of fashion. Gathered and fitted draping returns, over pink and cherry corselets on long evening gowns with full brown skirts. And then Valentino, quoting himself, sends his famous red down the runway. A perfect collection," Paola Pisa writes in the *Messaggero.*

"Twenty-five years of the Maison Valentino: the era of femininity. Valentino celebrates his twenty-fifth anniversary in fashion as only he would dare, with an epic production full of striking effects: a huge revolving curtain opens when pushed by delicate creatures who throw pearls to the audience while in the background the strains of *New York, New York* are heard. A group of artists and musicians from New York painted 'Valentino 25,' graffiti style, on the curtain and sang rap music while the models circled on the runway," *WWD* reports.

Valentino Che Veste di Nuovo comes out, a biography written by Marina Cosi and published by Camunia.

1985

Bettino Craxi, president of the Council of Ministers, inaugurates "L'Atelier dell'Illusione," an exhibition at the Castello Sforzesco in Milan, organized and produced by Valentino using costumes and designs representative of the Teatro alla Scala.

Spring–Summer Boutique: clean, bare lines that give the body importance and grace. Straight, short, clinging dresses. For the first time, shows officially at the Chambre de la Couture Française in Paris.

"Valentino: five-star Chic. Valentino, the Chic of Rome, slaked the fashion world's thirst, until then unsatisfied, with a five-star collection, a real knockout, characterized by sensuality without frivolity. Clearer, cleaner, and surprisingly sportier than ever, Valentino signals the 'sexy' message of the season without artifice, vulgarity, or hypocrisy," reports *WWD.*

June—honored as Grande Ufficiale dell'Ordine al Merito della Repubblica Italiana in Rome by President Sandro Pertini.

Designs Joan Collins's wardrobe for the TV series *Dynasty.*

Spring–Summer Couture: revisiting red and black in homage to Velázquez. "The final gown, of Taroni red silk fastened with two black velvet bows at the back, made the room go wild with applause. Other marvels were two dresses in the style of Velázquez's Infanta," Hebe Dorsey comments in the *International Herald Tribune.*

"They say that Milan is the capital of lyric opera, but the note of virtuosity was heard in Rome, when Valentino's silhouette took an astounding new direction, based on the idea of a high, in fact extremely high, waist," *WWD* reports.

"Gianni Agnelli has said that he is the biggest credit for Italy in the rest of the world. President Pertini added that he is the ambassador of Italian fashion to the world," writes Pia Soli in *Tempo.*

Fall–Winter Couture: slim, bare lines, without details, skirts to the knee, a lot of draping.

"Times have changed since Valentino's collections were considered a social offense by angry feminists who threw tomatoes at the elegant crowd and accused the designer of treating women as sex symbols. Today luxury is fashionable and Valentino is an institution. When he appeared on the runway at the conclusion of another triumphant collection, he displayed his latest honor, the Ordine al Merito della Repubblica Italiana, which had been conferred on him in June by outgoing President Sandro Pertini," Hebe Dorsey recounts in the *International Herald Tribune.*

1986

The new President of the Republic, Francesco Cossiga, bestows on Valentino the title of Cavaliere di Gran Croce.

A younger line is introduced, called Oliver, after his favorite dog.

Spring–Summer Boutique: characterized by simplicity, a line that clings to the body, short jackets, straight skirts, low heels.

"A fresh look, without frills: Valentino has come out with a collection of supreme purity, perhaps the most beautiful he has ever created. A hymn to beauty at its most rigorous," Hebe Dorsey comments in the *International Herald Tribune.*

"He exalts body consciousness, making it an art without using cheap expedients," writes *WWD.*

Designs the costumes for Lina Wertmüller's *Summer Night. . .* , with Mariangela Melato.

Spring–Summer Couture: wide jackets, shoulder yokes, short skirts. Soft, flowing dresses in polka-dot chiffon, embroidered gloves, chiffon scarves.

"While he uses embroidery generously—Fabergé designs on the bodice of a polka-dot chiffon dress—he can also astonish us with his simplicity, as in three breathtaking linen dresses in delicately blended shades of blue, sand, and jade," *WWD* reports.

Fall–Winter Boutique: wide capes with minuscule jacket-and-skirt outfits, a suggestion of Russia, Dandy coats with shawl collars in fur. "At the end of the day Valentino has shown that no one knows better how to create heart-stopping clothes," *WWD* says. "The week began with a beloved name: the great

Valentino. The closer the eccentricities and extravagances of fashion approach, the more we appreciate the restraint, the taste, the wisdom in Valentino's mix. His style is not intended to astonish," Lea Pericoli observes in the *Giornale Nuovo.* "Owning a Valentino is like owning a jersey dress by Madame Grès. Once you've bought it you can't let go of it. Women who own his clothes wear them for years. His influence is subtle—not shocking—but decisive. He was the first to show the sweater as evening wear or worn with a silk shirt and wool jacket. His chain print was widely imitated years ago, and his animal prints are bound to have legions of followers. And when buttons were the decorative detail, he sold loads of articles with them, and so did his imitators," Nina Hyde writes in the *Washington Post.*

Fall–Winter Couture: the silhouette is redesigned. Ankle-length skirts.

"And then came the turn of the master, Valentino, under the stars in Piazza Mignanelli. With spectacular effects of light, a hint of the subway in the surrounding windows, crowded with people, the elegant audience. On the runway the latest creations of the 'prophet' of Italian high fashion: generously proportioned calf-length skirts," Giuliana Ricca reports in the *Mattino.*

"Valentino uniquely loves to go against the current," Marina Cosi informs us in the *Giorno.* "Ever an exception, Valentino reinvents the new look," Pia Soli echoes in *Tempo.* "Valentino is always the undisputed leader in Italian fashion. . . . He closed his show by having 160 workers appear, all in white shirts, and he dedicated the public's ovation to them," writes Hebe Dorsey in the *International Herald Tribune.* "Piazza Mignanelli drowned in applause when the romantic chiffon evening gowns appeared, with careful workmanship inspired by the style of Jean Dessès, from whom the master of Italian fashion learned his skill. The draping required more than 45 yards of silk chiffon and more than 200 hours of work for a cost of around $15,000," explains *WWD.*

1987

Spring–Summer Boutique: a delicate, refined, romantic collection. Skirts are short. Terrorism is in the air at the Paris shows.

"To please the Americans, Valentino abandoned the tents and showed in an isolated, closely protected pavilion: and he had his usual triumph with a collection of touching elegance," Natalia Aspesi reports in the *Repubblica.*

Spring–summer Couture: a simple silhouette, clean, set off by a play of ruches and flounces.

"Valentino says: 'Women want to show off their bodies.' And no creator of fashion helps them do so better than Valentino. A youthful collection, with a lot of swing, and great attention to the tailoring details," *WWD* writes.

Fall–Winter Boutique: triangular line, with prominent shoulders, tiny, very short skirts, rounded jackets. Many animal prints. "Everyone was smiling after Valentino's show.... He is a happy man who knows his clients and what they expect of him. And he continues to make them happy with a bold beauty whose sole purpose is to make them more beautiful," Hebe Dorsey reports in the *International Herald Tribune.*

"These are the latest imperatives of the Italian designer who showed one of the most youthful, inventive, and diverting collections of recent years," Paola Pisa reports in the *Messaggero.*

Fall–Winter Couture: Valentino shows at Piazza Mignanelli with a collection of very short, sexy, youthful clothes.

"He himself, an audience of VIPs, and, scattered around or at the windows facing Piazza Mignanelli, attentive, cheering crowds gathered, thronging on foot and at the edges of the audience made up of kings and queens of the international world of theatre and finance, to enjoy elegant and moving creations that evoked the atmosphere of tales peopled with beautiful, buoyant women, standing on long legs, scantily dressed," Laura Griffo writes in *Nazione.*

"Valentino is at high voltage, with all the

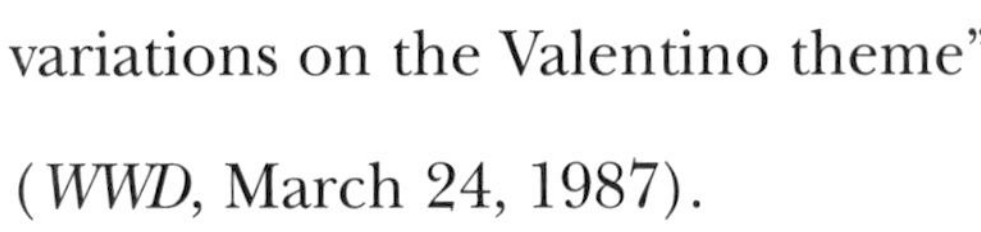

variations on the Valentino theme" (*WWD*, March 24, 1987).

September—Voghera invites its famous native son, organizing festivities in his honor that are attended by local authorities and theater personalities.

1988

Spring–Summer Boutique: a fresh, seductive grace, the body more hinted at than revealed in the lightness of the fabrics and a movement toward asymmetry. More animal prints, but mixed with plaids.

"Oh Valentino, so loved by women, adored by buyers, applauded by stern French journalists, what pleasure you give your faithful in the clothes of spring and summer. What balance, to shorten skirts in such a way that they are never immodest; what restraint, to put legs in cream-colored stockings and feet in beige shoes, so the display is never ostentatious; what sublime taste in the pairing of fabrics, what measured cheek in making her a little wild in those tiger stripes and leopard spots," eulogizes Paola Pisa in the *Messaggero.*

"It was a dark Monday. But Valentino's superlative taste and elegance saved the day. His sophistication allows him to speak the new language of fashion without any errors of pronunciation, as has happened to others," *WWD* writes.

"King of the fashion jungle, Valentino

offers his traditional spots for spring and summer. He has subdued the gold-spotted leopard, but has not tamed his 'op' zebra, especially when it's paired with zebra gloves, zebra beads, and zebra-frame eyeglasses," Nancy Hastings comments in the *Toronto Star.*

"Valentino at Bergdorf's is more a zoo than a boutique. Don't miss the chance to explore some of the most fascinating animal prints ever. Leopard legs emerge from leopard skirts. Patterns of tigers and leopards. Think of it as his refuge: he considers it one," the *New York Times* reports.

March—takes part in a show organized by ICE and by Domus Academy. "Italian fashion: creativity, technology, entrepreneurship in the Italian fashion industry." Valentino presents a tableau devoted to his "red."

May—Queen Sofia of Spain chooses a series of outfits from Valentino to wear during the visit of Queen Elizabeth of England to Madrid.

Valentino's Rome headquarters, 3500 square meters of Palazzo Mignanelli, are renovated.

Spring–Summer Couture: echoes of the commedia dell'arte, and Italian masks, in crinoline skirts and waist cintures, in the gaiety of eighteenth-century costumes.

"Valentino's arrival delivered a flickering image and brought back a shiver of creativity. King, ruler, emperor, with all the weight of the legend that surrounds him, Valentino presented an enclosure stupendously decorated in trompe-l'œil as a joyful dreamlike Italian garden. It was a successful performance of authentic Haute Couture. What Valentino showed Thursday evening inspired the sensation of a second creative youth that, joined to the total mastery of the skills and the marvel of materials and workmanship, brings Italian Couture to truly international levels," writes Adriana Mulassano in *Corriere della Sera.*

The advertising campaign consists of 24 large photographs, and is called "Valeografie."

Fall–Winter Boutique: the triumph of decoration: rosettes, braid, embroidery inspired by Aubusson carpets.

"Anyone who owns an Aubusson may be puzzled by the notion of wearing one. But women who do not will certainly be eager to finally have an Aubusson, with flowers and spirals, woven into jackets and cashmere sweaters, or embroidered on the big skirts of evening gowns, or hand-painted, by skilled artisans, on light wool jackets," Natalia Aspesi reports in the *Repubblica.*

"Exit, applause: so it went for the whole collection. The record is held by Valentino in this Olympiad of French fashion, which ended today," Lucia Mari writes in *Giorno.*

Fall–Winter Couture: an aristocratic fitted torso opens into a feminine pleat of refined simplicity.

"None of the images of woman proposed for Fall–Winter 1988-89 is as subtle, as mysterious as Valentino's. A woman faces the cold in a slender tapered redingote, shaped at most in the bust and perhaps also from the waist to the hem, stopping at the calf; but the sunburst or accordion pleat, barely rustling when there is no movement to animate it, transforms the purity of the cut into energy, rhythm, and supple vitality," Lucia Sollazzo observes in the *Stampa*.
November—shows in Los Angeles. "Valentino was the hero of a gala evening whose proceeds were given entirely to the children's Institute Against Child Abuse (an international organization that fights against abuse of any kind in childhood). The event—to which RAI Uno devoted a Christmas Day special—took place in the legendary Twentieth Century Fox studios, and present were VIPs old and new, including Anjelica Huston, Gregory Peck, John Travolta, Sidney Poitier, Joan Collins, George Hamilton, Walter Matthau, Morgan Fairchild, Quincy Jones, and Linda Evans," reports *Giorno*.
The mayor of Beverly Hills, Robert Tannenbaum, organizes a Valentino Day and gives the couturier the gold keys to the city.
"Like a Caesar of our time, Valentino 'came, saw, and conquered,' in a visit to Los Angeles that lasted a weekend," writes *WWD*.

1989

Spring–Summer Boutique: a collection inspired by India and, in particular, Madras.
"Valentino the Magnificent. Sumptuousness and simplicity: a marriage of love celebrated by Valentino, who treats the most expensive materials in a sporty, casual manner," writes Janie Samet in *Le Figaro*.
January—decides to present his Couture collections in Paris again, in spite of the polemics.
Spring–Summer Couture: a narrow silhouette, almost military, long jackets, wide pants. Wrap coats in black or white.
"Valentino shook off the Roman shows with an unassailable spring collection, leaving polemics on the sidelines. This is what Valentino knows best: keeping everything under control. With a solid sense of proportion and a steady hand for details," observes Mark Ganem in *WWD*.
"French women turn their eyes heavenward in an attitude of desire, calling Valentino, here known as the magnificent, Lorenzo de' Medici," Lucia Sollazzo reports in the *Stampa*.
"Valentino presented his Couture collection in Paris for the first time. His elegant, feminine line demonstrates that the best Italian fashion can compete with the most sophisticated peaks of the French," Bernadine Morris says in the *New York Times*.

Fall–Winter Boutique: quilting and patchwork. The eveningwear is a Renaissance portrait, in black velvets set off by large bunches of white lace at the throat.

"Ah, that picture. One cannot take one's eyes off Valentino. Of course, it's on a wall of his studio, it was painted by Bronzino and is a portrait of Eleonora of Toledo. What an inspiration, the clothes perfectly imitate the grande dame: white collars like gorgets adorn shirts and black velvet dresses of masterly workmanship; gilded nets overlay sleeves and shoulders, and reveal the whole back through the lightest evening clothes at the Palazzo. On other bodices are beads, baroque black embroidery, and jewel-buttons," Paola Pisa reports in the *Messaggero.*

"The Toscanini of elegance," decrees Janie Samet of *Le Figaro.*

Fall–Winter Couture: a collection inspired by the work of Hoffmann and the Wiener Werkstätte, destined to live in the history of fashion. Also, the Accademia Valentino opens a new headquarters for shows and exhibits in a building restored by Valentino. The collection is presented later in Paris at the Théâtre de Chaillot. "Valentino has been inspired by a vigorous artistic movement, the Wiener Werkstätte, and has adapted its geometric themes to contemporary fashion. The motifs of furniture and architecture have been skillfully transposed to sweaters, blazers,

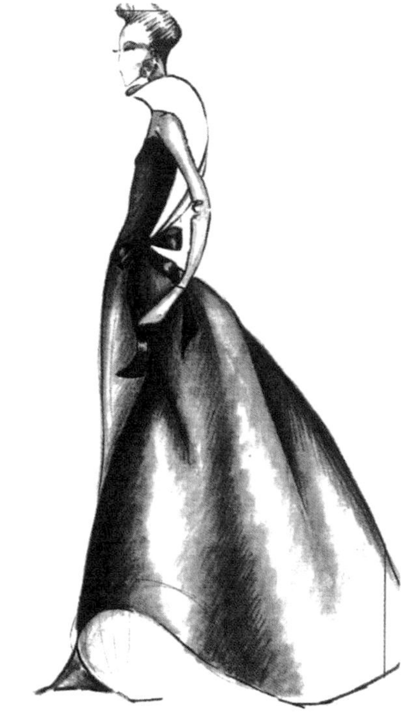

and evening gowns. The result is a powerful look that clearly distances them from the flowers and plaids that are normally seen in fashion," writes Bernadine Morris in the *New York Times.*

A fashion designer wanders the world, visits museums, gets to know different peoples and customs, and, like everyone, is exposed to suggestions and emotions, and can travel as he pleases in time and space. What distinguishes him from others is that, as for every artist, these occasions lose their casualness by acquiring an intimate necessity.

"Thus Valentino's encounter with the art of the Vienna Secession, of a Hoffmann or of a Kilo Moser, is the source of today's collection, in which neo-Hellenic and neo-Byzantine graphic elements and motifs from the Wiener Werkstätte have been transported to suits, coats, and dresses," Laura Dubini observes in the *Corriere della Sera.*

"But what bears even more resemblance to the Wiener Werkstätte is Valentino's plan to take over, beyond the show, the eighteenth-century premises of the former Accademia di Belle Arti, which had been used for sculpture studios. This would provide space for his own archives, in view of the thirtieth anniversary of his house (in 1990), and space for public shows of artistic events that might otherwise be relegated to the private and unobserved: a painting, a film that can't circulate, a play, a book, an object: a Romische Werkstätte?" Rita Cirio comments in *Espresso.*

October—receives in Washington, in the presence of President Francesco Cossiga, the prestigious N.I.A.F. prize in recognition of his "inestimable contribution to fashion in the last thirty years."

1990

Spring–Summer Boutique: flowers burst forth, polka dots, animal prints, black and white stripes, in a collection based on foulards, knotted at the chest or around the hips.

"More glory for an Italian in Paris: it is Valentino, who yesterday afternoon showed the French the tricks and caprices of his fragile yet imperious woman," Laura Laurenzi notes in the *Repubblica.*

Spring–Summer Couture: the Accademia Valentino officially opens in Rome, with Giancarlo Giammetti as president, and L.I.F.E. is introduced, the organization pledged to the fight against AIDS, sponsored by Elizabeth Taylor, who is present at the opening. A show on the Roman school serves as the background for a preview of the Spring–Summer models, which in color and line recall the famous white collection of 1968. The cultural activities of the Academy continue, in May, with the prestigious traveling show "The Art of Cartier," which opened in Paris at the Petit-Palais in 1989.

"It was a slight disappointment for the eight hundred special guests of Valentino. Thursday evening, the Academy that bears the name of the great designer who has now deserted Rome for Paris opened, and with it, an extraordinary show of paintings and sculpture of the Roman School opened (and closed that same night), but the cream of Italic society who knocked at Piazza Mignanelli was in reality animated by a different desire, that is, to see Elizabeth Taylor in person—a privilege that was granted to very few," Laura Laurenzi reports in the *Repubblica.*

"Although the Roman public was able to taste only a small portion—twenty models—of his entire Couture menu, it was an extremely appetizing aperitif, and almost entirely in the color favored by Valentino this season: white. Only the final model, a chiffon gown with bare shoulders and a flounced skirt, was in the traditional, vivid 'Valentino red,'" *WWD* reports.

Paris—the entire collection is shown at the Théâtre de Chaillot, which was transformed into an Italian terrace overlooking the Mediterranean.

"'No more extravagance,' Valentino declared after presenting a summer collection that was light as a feather. In the background was a view of a columned terrace overlooking the sea,"

Suzy Menkes writes in the *International Herald Tribune.*

"As a couturier here in Paris he gave a demonstration of rigor and strength. No artifice, no quotations or homages, every inspiration translated into terms of pure Couture. One could say that Valentino's collection was devoted to the art itself of creating Haute Couture clothes," Laura Dubini observes in the *Corriere della Sera.*

Designs the wedding dress for the Archduchess Sophia of Hapsburg, who is to marry Prince Hugo Windisch-Grätz.

April—arranges a show at the Hotel Savoy in London, attended by Princess Diana, on behalf of the AIDS Crisis Trust, an English organization with which he establishes a partnership, contributing to the construction, in Scotland, of the first center for victims of AIDS.

Fall–Winter Boutique: inspired by Etruscan art.

"Valentino, who has long been interested in research into what was once considered a minor art, has gone back to the *buccheri,* the Etruscan vases, and given their colors, terra-cotta and black, ivory and brown, and designs to his exquisite winter collection: the Etruscan profiles, the rearing horses, the graphic elements of Greek keys and spirals," Lucia Sollazzo writes in the *Stampa.*

"Valentino has borrowed the decorations of Etruscan vases for clothes that nevertheless succeed in displaying a contemporary look," declares Bernadine Morris in the *New York Times.*

"Valentino appeared in a state of grace. He is on the threshold of the thirtieth year of work and is preparing an exhibit of the important periods of his stylistic journey, which will open next January at the Accademia Valentino, in the renovated Palazzo Mignanelli," Lucia Sollazzo adds in the *Stampa.*

"While he was searching the archives for materials for his retrospective, which will be seen in Rome and then elsewhere in the world, Valentino found an evening gown with draping on one shoulder that he had created for Jacqueline Kennedy in 1965. He remade it in pine-green satin, and the elegance and simplicity of that dress stood out in a sea of decoration. It could even be a sign of change," Suzy Menkes reveals in the *International Herald Tribune.*

July—on the television spectacular *Under the Stars,* Ornella Muti appears in a historic dress: the sheath in red crêpe of 1964. The exhibit "Valentino. Thirty Years of Magic" is announced.

On the occasion of President Francesco Cossiga's visit to England, the Victoria and Albert Museum displays some dresses by Valentino that he personally shows Queen Elizabeth.

November—Valentino's largest boutique, more than 3000 square feet devoted to the Valentino Boutique lines, opens at 2 Rodeo Drive in Los Angeles. "The propensity of Chic for luxury is evident in the 3000 square feet of the store, which cost more than two million dollars. It's hard to say which was more brilliant, the invitation list—packed with names like Swifty and Mary Lazar, Sylvester Stallone, Barbara Davis, Barry Diller, and beauties like Marisa Berenson, Jane Seymour, and Ornella Muti (all in Valentino)—or the sumptuous decoration of the store, with its mirrored columns, inlaid wood, teak, parchment-covered walls, chrome, and permanent, standard-length runway," writes *WWD* the day after the opening.

December—at the Milan headquarters on Via Brera, Federico Zeri introduces the book *Valentino. Thirty Years of Magic* by Marie-Paule Pellé, with essays by other well-known writers, published by Leonardo Arte and Abbeville Press.

Decides to put off the "Thirty Years of Magic" show until June, 1991 because of the international situation resulting from the Gulf War.

1991

Spring–Summer Couture:

Valentino's collection, shown at the Musée des Arts Décoratifs in Paris, recalls the early sixties, with short, straight skirts for day and evening, along with tulip-shaped skirts. Fine fabrics and embroidery are featured for evening and black and white are leading players everywhere. "A bracing wind from the sixties blows over Valentino's runway" is the headline in *WWD*.

"Valentino has presented a collection that, after a score of daytime outfits, introduced an infinite series of cocktail and evening dresses that were a triumph of elaborate decoration," Silvia Giacomoni reports in the *Repubblica*.

"Delicate femininity, perfection of execution, a discreetly drawn silhouette: in short, seduction without revolution. A marvelous show and a splendid demonstration of savoir-faire, for the pampered woman who wants to be known for an elegance that is more exceptional than innovative," Janie Samet comments in *Le Figaro*.

"In his thirty-year career, Valentino has learned all the tricks of fashion—cut, detail, craftsmanship... for him everything has to be perfect," Suzy Menkes concludes in the *International Herald Tribune*. The show's finale is a floor-length white silk dress with the word "peace" embroidered on it in many languages: Italian, Hungarian, Spanish, Greek, English, Arabic, German, Russian, Polish, Hebrew, French, Egyptian, Dutch, Indian, and, on the gloves, Japanese.

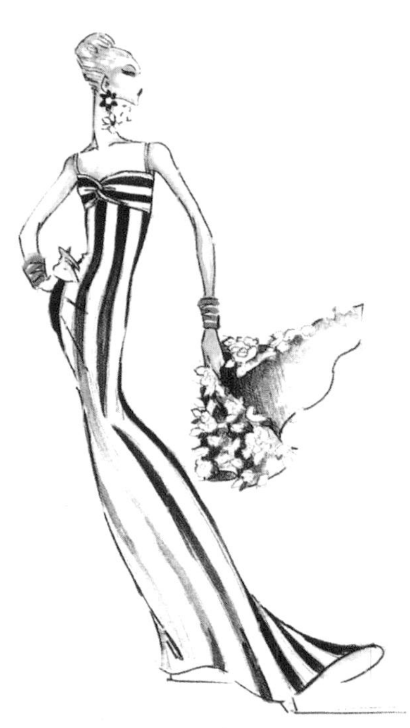

Sophia Loren receives the Academy Award for lifetime achievement at the Dorothy Chandler Pavilion in Los Angeles, and Valentino designs a tight-fitting low-necked black lace dress for the actress to wear at the ceremony.

June—inaugurates the festivities—announced, postponed, in long preparation—in honor of his thirty years of activity.

June 6th—opens the show "Thirty Years of Magic: The Images," at the Capitoline Museum, an exhibition with contributions from sixty of the most famous draftsmen and photographers in the world. The made-for-television film by Frédéric Mitterrand is shown in previews at the Campidoglio, and Franco Carraro, the mayor of Rome, holds a reception on the terrace of Villa Cattarelli. The next day, at the Accademia Valentino, the designer cuts the ribbon at the show "Thirty Years of Magic: The Works," an anthology of more than three hundred outfits from 1960 to 1990 that tell the story of Valentino's passions. Finally, a breakfast is held at the Casina Valadier and a gala dinner at the Villa Medici for six hundred invited guests. Attending the festivities are colleagues and friends from all over the world: ElizabethTaylor, Gianni and Marella Agnelli, Nancy Kissinger, Mikhail Baryshnikov, Ornella Muti, Ira von Fürstenberg, Marina di Savoia, Ivana Trump, and many others.

Takes the opportunity to present his new perfume for women: Vendetta.

Fall–Winter Couture: the collection is characterized by a clear return to true Haute Couture, as evidenced by workmanship and attention to detail. A lot of red, a lot of black, narrow ruching, flounces, amusing spirals. Tulle comes back in a big way, recalling Valentino's earliest collections, in the late fifties. The grand finale of the show is a long, clinging evening gown, with large roses at the hem, worn under an immense evening cape of white satin with hand-painted pink brushstrokes. "Valentino declares that the elegant woman of the winter of 1991-92 will look like the women portrayed by the photographer Cecil Beaton," writes the *Messaggero.*

"It was a triumph for Valentino, the Prince Charming of the wealthiest and most beautiful women in the world. Adored by the international jet set, Valentino was hailed as the absolute star of the day," Claire Roberts observes on *Today.*

"Sublime Valentino. To his thirty years of magic another day is added: the collection that he presented on Wednesday, which marked the end of the Haute Couture shows for winter 1991-92, is indeed magical.

This certified high-quality designer has never been so good: he was enthusiastically applauded by Sandra Attolico, wife of the Italian ambassador to France, Pat Kennedy, Cristina Piaggio, by many women who have royal pedigrees and others who are merely rich; all of them, however, have the means to buy an exclusive, signature dress, to display like the coat of arms on a visiting card, the Picasso in the living room, the Ferrari in front of the house," comments Lucia Mari in the *Giorno.*
Fall–Winter Boutique: the collection has a slight flavor of the nineteenth century, with new *bombé* lines swelling over the hips, accented by a narrow waist and more natural-looking shoulders, worn with high chamois boots. A lot of English and Welsh tweed for day, rich velvets and brocades for evening. Another significant theme is the riding jacket, the redingote that hugs the hips. "Valentino has lavished enthusiasm, color, and brio on his collection,and it was received with ecstatic applause," Laura Dubini writes in the *Corriere della Sera.* She continues, "A Valentino, therefore, who is particularly eclectic and eager to give a little shake-up, to provoke his faithful clientele. His woman is now ready to put on her new boots, embellished by a bow, to wear sheepskin decorated with designs typical of Kilim carpets, to almost always dress in a single color: now all in tangerine, now blue from head to toe, now lilac,

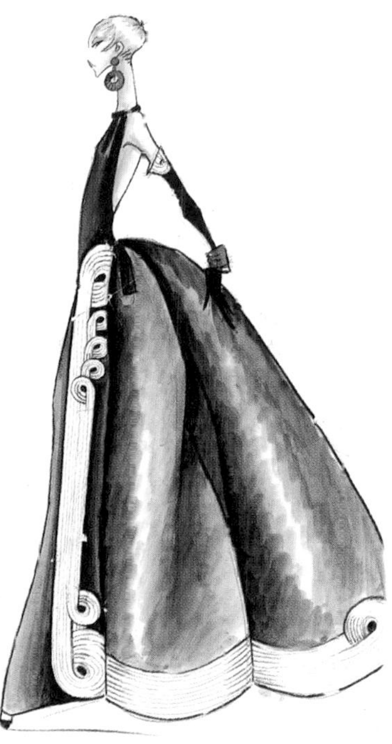

sunflower, green, black."
"Of all the designers who presented their collections, Valentino was the best. There were still no earth movers in his collection, but no weaknesses, either. In an ingenious way, he simply reworked his Couture hits," Paula Reed writes in the *Sunday Times.*
October—Elizabeth Taylor marries for the eighth time. Valentino, her close friend, who is to design her wedding dress, creates a classic silhouette: full skirt with a tight bodice of palest yellow embellished with a lace guipure inspired by the sixteenth century.
November—the heads of state and government of the sixteen member nations of NATO convene at an extraordinary summit in Rome. The First Ladies visit the show "Valentino: Thirty Years of Magic," accompanied by the couturier himself. "Atlantic First Ladies Bewitched by Valentino. The designer's outfits score a greater success than *Rigoletto*" is Marina Mastroluca's headline in the *Unità* the next day.

1992

Spring–Summer Couture: At the École des Beaux-Arts Valentino presents a collection inspired by the

twenties, the jazz age, characters in the novels of F. Scott Fitzgerald. Low-waisted dresses with a straight but shimmying line, slits, pleated hemline. The colors are those of eighteenth-century paintings: cloud white, sky blue, dawn and sunset pink. "For Valentino sensuality returns to bourgeois concealment, becoming discreet, coy. It is there, but must not be visible at first glance," Paola Pisa writes in the *Messaggero.* And she adds: "Valentino is justly proud of this collection, which brings back into the wardrobe the sweetest aspect of femininity. 'Stunning!' is the comment of the women in the audience." "The Italian couturier Valentino has put on a show that clearly separates fantasy from reality. Fantasy: Ming vases embroidered in sequins and rhinestones on jackets and skirts, cherry blossoms and pagodas printed on beige and brown silks. Reality: white or navy wool suits with delicate white collars," Bernadine Morris writes in the *New York Times.*
Spring–Summer Boutique: this collection is almost like a game of elements. The elements open and close, grow long and short, disguise themselves to reveal different lengths, different dynamics, and contradictory lines. Dresses with the same cut are made in both long and short versions, to demonstrate the

immutable perfection of the proportions; dresses as straight as pencil leads have flared, lively, dancing skirts with a flowerlike cut. "Long or short, this is not a problem for Valentino, the master of elegance. Long skirts open over a lace-edged underskirt. Pleated skirts allow a glimpse of a pair of shorts. Long peasant dresses reveal baby-doll pajamas underneath. The outer layer that draws attention to what is beneath it through a play of transparencies and openings," Claudine Hesse writes enthusiastically in *Le Figaro.*
"Valentino has made a conquest of the Paris audience, which at the end of the show gave him a standing ovation, the highest tribute a designer can receive," Paola Pisa writes in the *Messaggero.*
"Valentino played his winning card in the delicate, romantic atmosphere that pervaded his show. It is an atmosphere that may at times be too studied, but is always extremely charming," Hillary Alexander observes in the *Daily Telegraph.*
March—at the Academy Awards in Los Angeles, Valentino dresses Susan Sarandon, nominated for *Thelma and Louise,* and Bette Midler, Mercedes Ruehl, Jessica Tandy, Elizabeth Taylor, and Nicole Kidman.

Fall–Winter Couture: the entire collection of eighty-eight outfits is inspired by the forties and by such painters as Gustav Klimt. It includes many dresses in black and gold, with exquisite embroideries and ribbons woven to create grids, lines, lozenges, fantastic insects; there are long jackets in the style of the white telephone divas, calf-length skirts that widen into a flare. The models all have their hair waved, Gilda-style, and on their heads they wear berets and embroidered cloches.

"Valentino takes Paris again" is Paola Pisa's headline in the *Messaggero.* And she goes on: "It would be impossible to describe all the ensembles, eighty-eight of them, each more beautiful than the last, more seductive, more sophisticated. 'What marvelous clothes!' comment Joan Collins and Ivana Trump, who are present at this spectacular show, along with billionaire Arabs, sitting, as if on an ocean liner, at ninety small tables with only candles for illumination."

Fall–Winter Boutique: brings back the animal print, with variegated fabrics and brocades, ribbons and feathers that lend opulence to exceptional coats and long capes. Passementerie cords are the key for getting from morning to evening and are seen in suits with pearl-embroidered sleeves, braid, and tassels, and in necklines like Anita Ekberg's just before she dives into the Trevi Fountain.

"Valentino knows the recipe for seducing women extremely well. He is passionate about all things precious and delicate: lace blouses, white pleated plastrons with insets of Valenciennes lace, organ-pipe hems, rhinestone embroidery on black jackets, organza married to velvet," Janie Samet observes in *Le Figaro.*

"Valentino has stunned Paris with designs inspired by the rebellion in Sherwood Forest," Lucia Sollazzo writes in the *Stampa.*

"Valentino's exuberant collection, which got a warm welcome, sends Robin Hood's band out onto the runway, along with a modern Lady Rowena of Ivanhoe and a delightful pagegirl," recounts Laura Dubini in the *Corriere della Sera.* And she goes on to observe: "Luxury gives no sign of recession here."

September—celebrates his thirtieth anniversary in New York, where the Park Avenue Armory, the immense, legendary home of the Seventh Regiment, is host to the show "Thirty Years of Magic." Many illustrious guests attend the opening, from Sophia Loren to Matilda Cuomo, from Ivana Trump to Elizabeth Taylor, Susan Sarandon, designer friends (Calvin Klein, Ralph Lauren, Donna Karan, Oscar de la Renta), the most famous models in the world (Linda Evangelista, Claudia Schiffer, Christy Turlington, Yasmeen Ghauri, Karen Mulder, Nadège). An improvised trio made up of Placido Domingo, Bette Midler, and Aretha Franklin sings *Happy Anniversary to You* to Valentino.

The exhibition, organized in connection with the celebrations of the cinquecentennial of the discovery of America, reports more than 70,000 visitors in less than two weeks.

November—the show "Seduction from Boucher to Warhol" opens at the Accademia Valentino, including more than sixty fine paintings from museums and private collections all over the world.

1993

Spring–Summer Couture: The woman of the year 2000 introduced in Paris has abandoned the businesslike, managerial look and turned to the romantic. Soft, delicate, slender, without ostentation, she approaches the runway on tiptoe, counting on her femininity alone.

"Forget the froufrou. Even Valentino chooses the *delicato* for next season," admonishes *WWD*. The designer

himself explains, in presenting his collection: "Everything is light, delicate, soft. There is nothing harsh or heavy."

"Valentino suggests a subtle, romantic elegance, composed of pareo-style skirts and blouses as close-fitting as gloves, of evening gowns as impalpable as clouds. Chic? It is a long dark jumper enlivened by a little pale-colored blouse, or a vest worn with a flounced skirt. And then there is the jewel dress, which took a hundred and forty hours to produce: 110 yards of white chiffon, for the evening costume that ends in a thousand fringes," Antonella Amapane reports in the *Stampa*.

"In the first row: Princess Firyal of Jordan, Marina Cicogna, Marella Agnelli, Cristina Piaggio, Marie-Hélène de Rothschild, Marina of Greece with her daughters Alexandra and Olga. All of them clients of Haute Couture," Lea Pericoli writes in the *Giornale*.

Spring–Summer Boutique: Valentino's collection emphasizes the new dimensions that lengthen hems to the calf, make jackets shorter and tighter, feature camisoles in a game of "now you see it, now you don't" played with wearable transparencies. Trousers offer variations with three pleated flounces and sunburst lines that lengthen any figure.

"Valentino takes as his subject Africa, a continent that fascinates him and gives him the opportunity to highlight those burned tones he loves so much. Using the abstract designs of Kenya in combination with elephant and other animal designs, he has fashioned a collection that is both coherent and very beautiful," Bernadine Morris writes in the *New York Times.*

"Valentino's African queen wears light fabrics printed with tribal patterns that are often accented by embroidery," writes Pia Soli in *Tempo.* And she goes on: "One of Valentino's oldest fans, Oscar de la Renta, joined in the applause."

May—is invited to Beijing by the Chinese government to inaugurate "Chic '93," a large Asian exhibition of textiles, by presenting his Fall–Winter 1993–94 Prêt-à-porter collection. "The couturier sent the twelve hundred invited guests at the China World Trade Hotel into raptures," writes the *Messaggero.* Valentino is welcomed personally by Jiang Zemin, President of the Chinese Republic.

1994

January—the opera *The Dream of Valentino* has its première in Washington. Written by Dominick Argento, the work tells the story of the legendary silent-movie star Rudolf Valentino, the White Sheik. Designs the costumes for the twenty-seven main characters and the hundred and thirty extras.

"Valentino for Valentino. A myth of today for a myth of the past," Laura Dubini writes in the *Corriere della Sera.*

Spring–Summer Couture: a collection based entirely on lace. Shown at the Grand Hôtel, the collection includes fine silk lace in the style of the late nineteenth century and coarse rustic lace, a lot of chiffon, and slips entirely of different kinds of lace.

"Valentino, the best in Paris, thrilled the audience with dresses of two or three layers of the palest chiffon," Paola Pisa writes in *Il Messaggero.*

"Valentino came from Rome to teach the French a few things about delicacy and craftsmanship in the construction of Couture clothes. And this was one of his better moments," Bernardine Morris comments in the *International Herald Tribune.*

"A beautiful, rich, very refined collection, which offers true pleasure while so many are destroying Haute Couture," observes Monsieur Lesage, who provided the marvelous embroidery that is brilliantly displayed on the runway.

"Valentino's show took place in an eager silence punctuated by restrained clapping. Gratitude was expressed at the end with a huge round of applause and cries of enthusiasm. The women who cheered Valentino have no desire to try new fashions, new dimensions. From Haute Couture they ask only the inimitable. And it is Valentino who gives it to them," Silvia Giacomoni comments in the *Repubblica*.

"If seduction is your game, then Valentino is your couturier," *WWD* decrees.

Spring–Summer Boutique: The finale of Valentino's show was Sharon Stone, who came down the runway in a short, witty wedding dress. "No one manages to seduce like Valentino, and no one dresses a woman in such a seductive manner. Valentino has given something fresh and nonchalant to next season's lingerie look, creating one of the simplest and at the same time richest collections of the Paris shows," WWD reports.

March—at the Academy Awards ceremony, Tom Hanks, Sharon Stone, Debra Winger, Al Pacino, and Nicole Kidman wear Valentino.

Takes part in Convivio, a benefit organized at the Milan Triennial on behalf of ANLAIDS (National Organization for the Fight Against AIDS), which previews a sort of luxury shopping center, where one can buy dresses and other products of the most celebrated fashion houses at special prices.

Fall–Winter Couture: Valentino incorporates allusions to camouflage, with Army-green General Patton-style mohair coats, berets, elasticized boots that fit like stockings, alternating with silk evening suits in with camouflage patterns and short black dresses with flared, swinging skirts.

"Wonderful!" exclaims Joan Collins. "The faithless Alexis is right," Paola Pisa confirms in the *Messaggero*, "because no other adjective better explains Valentino's Haute Couture: he always has one more gear, that of femininity."

"Valentino balanced on the style fence with more grace than most. There were lunching suits, sober little tweed numbers with A-line skirts and elegant crêpe evening dresses by the bucketful for conservative taste, but the scene-stealers were the funky crinolines cut in khaki," Paula Reed reports in the *Sunday Times*.

Fall–Winter Boutique: the collection, presented in the rooms of the Carrousel du Louvre, in Paris, recalls the atmosphere of the film *The Piano*. Offerings in the total black look are exquisite: straight bodices with a starched child's collar, white schoolgirlish accents, *bon chic bon genre* pleated skirts that reveal, like a jack-in-the-box, startling provocative lace slips, skin-tight dresses decorated with arabesques, boots trimmed in gold.

"The most glamorous show of the week was Valentino's. Even if his clothes were in somber shades (mostly black and chocolate), lightened by flashes of grain color, ivory and red, the designer chose understatement," Iain Webb comments in the *Times*.

October–the exhibit "Italian Metamorphosis," assembled by Germano Celant, opens at the Guggenheim Museum in New York. On display are twenty-five years of Italian creativity, from 1943 to 1968, as expressed in art, cinema, photography, fashion, architecture, and design. Some of Valentino's most sumptuous creations are shown in the section devoted to fashion.

1995

January—Florence celebrates Valentino's return with a show held at the Stazione Leopolda, thirty years after the designer's first show presented at the Pitti Palace. The mayor of Florence confers on Valentino a special prize for artistic merit in the field of fashion.

Spring–Summer Couture: the collection, shown at the Grand Hôtel in Paris, is inspired by the great classics of forty years earlier yet attentive to the current reality of a sophisticated, twenty-first-century look. The miniskirt is totally abandoned. The new suits have sleeveless jackets, a small bow at the breast, waists accented by darts, a masterly cut, and skirts that graze the knee. The dresses, with rounded lines and careful detailing, have drapings of black tulle; underskirts for evening in pale icy colors are embellished by lace inserts.

"Valentino bewitches Paris" is the headline of the international press. Among those who applauded the show, including both wealthy buyers and a happy public, were Monica Bellucci and Rupert Everett next to Sao Schlumberger, Marisa Berenson, Lilian Rossi di Montelera, Prince Laurent of Belgium, Princess Marina of Greece and her daughter Olga, the conductor David Oren with his beautiful wife, and Madame Clerico, the owner of the "Lido." Elegance, refinement, luxury, charm, and great Couture. Valentino has conquered Paris. The couturier scored a hit from the very first design," Laura Dubini reports in the *Corriere della Sera*. At the show, Sharon Stone and Jessica Lang "reserve" from the designer the dresses they will wear to the Academy Awards, in Los Angeles in March.

Spring–Summer Boutique: the dresses that make up the new collection are sober, without excess. Many imitation-rustic wools, airy sequins for day and night, a touch of marabou, long white siren-style dresses, with subtle transparencies, crinolines with dozens of petticoats, undulating printed saris.

"The collection is a challenge to Prêt-à-porter with its luxury and refinements offered to women who are certainly rich and famous, dressed in white linen and opalescent chiffon, precious suits with richly-draped skirts. In this field Valentino is a real *virtuoso,*" Janie Samet reports in *Le Figaro.*

"For daily life where charming surprises are expected, for evenings where the feminine utterly dominates, Valentino has used the same plan: a bodice with straps laced over a corselet under a faultless jacket, a knee-length skirt or short but never exhibitionist shorts. After the show, which was greeted by cheers, the women rushed backstage and rained kisses on him, without discomposing his calm elegance," Natalia Aspesi writes in the *Repubblica.* "A really exceptional collection," says Marina of Savoy. "This is true Italian glamour,"

declares Valentino's fellow-designer Vivienne Westwood, who attended the show. "Aristocratic kisses, prestigious embraces, dozens of television crews and photographers. Barely a minute after the show ended everyone was pushing and shoving to get backstage," Paola Pisa reports in the *Messaggero.*

Designs a wedding dress for Marie-Chantal Miller, who marries Paul of Greece in London.

Fall–Winter Couture: the collection presented at the Grand Hôtel in Paris causes a sensation because of its obvious intention to express seductiveness in a manner unusually explicit in the designer's canon. The show opens with a nude male clasping the slender, arrowlike form of a gorgeous model who shows off her marvelous body through a long slit in her orchid-pink gown. "A legendary embrace. A legendary nude. Adam and Eve enter the history of Haute Couture. And it is a sudden shock, extremely pleasant and unusual, for those who attend the stuffy shows of Paris Haute Couture," Eva Desiderio writes in *Nazione.*

Giancarlo Giammetti explains, with a smile: "Every so often Haute Couture needs a feather duster to clear away some of the cobwebs that have accumulated over the years."

"We are in Valentino's paradise, in a

tropical forest that climbs up onto the gilded runway," Laura Dubini explains in the *Corriere della Sera.* Indeed, the collection has drawn inspiration from the colors and shapes of tropical flowers charged with sensuality and erotic significance: long dresses of purple, lilac, intense pink, short satin pareos wrapped around black sheath dresses, chiffon spirals.

Fall–Winter Boutique: the theme of the collection is retro chic, and it invites its clients to fantasize as they turn the pages of a fashion magazine of many years ago, or rummage in their grandmother's trunk. Retro chic, then: beautiful ankle-length coats with a masculine cut, trousers with cuffs, softened by a pullover, or a shiny blouse, crossed and knotted behind. Often there is the touch of a scarf, of cuffs, of a fake-fur collar. Evening clothes concentrate on white, in all its tonalities, from ivory to ice.

December—the Accademia Valentino is host to the archeological exhibit "The Mystery of a Young Girl," centering on the ancient tomb of a young woman that was discovered in Rome.

1996

Spring–Summer Couture: shows a delicate, sophisticated collection in the foyer of the Paris Opera. The dresses have a slender, graceful silhouette and are in mild pastel colors, with extraordinary workmanship. The artistry of his atelier is manifest in exquisite dresses of tulle and lace patchwork, in enchanting short mesh jackets made of little tubes and inspired by ancient Japanese kimonos, in delicate *tenues de soirées,* almost like slips, embroidered with beads. Also, the lace stockings shown in 1968 with the famous white collection are brought back in pastel colors. "A lesson in simplicity," the designer himself explains.

Spring–Summer Boutique: introduces a subtle, exuberant line: chiffon skirts long and slim or with flounces; short sweaters with sailor stripes and caban jackets of heavy jersey. For evening remarkable dresses embroidered with shell and starfish motifs, with satin petticoats tied on the side like a pareo.

"Valentino dresses beautiful women, never undressing them: his transparencies are subtle," Janie Samet observes in *Le Figaro.* "Valentino brings back the *charme* of the elegant woman," Eva Desiderio writes in the *Nazione.* And she adds: "Valentino's was a show for the eyes and for the heart; according to recent polls he is the best known designer in the world."

The Accademia Valentino is the site

chosen to present to the public the celebrated Codex Leicester of Leonardo da Vinci.

April—John Kennedy, Jr., passing through Rome, visits the exhibit and gives his support to the benefit "A Hundred Dinners for L.I.F.E." by attending the first dinner.

June—Valentino is named Cavaliere del Lavoro by the President of the Italian Republic, Oscar Luigi Scalfaro.

Fall–Winter Couture: a collection whose theme is the woman of mystery. Quickness, Concision, Exactitude, Lightness, Multiplicity, the paradigms of Italo Calvino's *Six Memos for the Next Millennium*, form the thread that allows one to "read" the show comprehensively.

Quickness in the vertical silhouette of rigorously longuette dresses. Concision in the exquisitely elemental evening slips of georgette, chiffon, muslin. Exactitude in the proportions of the deep necklines tapering into tiny shoulder straps. Lightness in the lace trimmings and in narrow collars of expensive fur. Multiplicity in the fashion details, like narrow belts, sometimes simple, sometimes studded with beads or rhinestones.

Fall–Winter Boutique: on the runway a collection that plays on the vivacity and the joie de vivre of the casual modern woman, in seductive but not

provocative skirts of three layers of chiffon, and at the same time in almost masculine clothes, for example a white shirt with ruching, or a slim suit with a high-necked jacket and severe trousers.

"At Valentino the seductiveness of the year 2000 is on parade," writes Laura Asnaghi in the *Repubblica*. And she explains: "In Valentino's clothes everything is finely calibrated. Short, knee-length coats are worn with sophisticated hats of marabou, black skirts sport beaded belts, and jumpsuits for daytime are slim, intended for women of reedlike thinness. Night is definitely more sinful, with transparent materials, embroidery, and veils." Finally, she concludes, "Valentino wants to make women happy." "Valentino conquers Paris again," Paola Pollo declares in the *Corriere della Sera*. She continues: "A hundred and forty outfits, without a break in femininity: neither angels nor sexy dolls but women who are happy."

September—inaugurates a new one-thousand-square-foot store on Madison Avenue in New York, which replaces his previous store. Also in September, the first Fashion Biennial opens in Florence, curated by Germano Celant, Luigi Settembrini, and Ingrid Sischy. Valentino is among thirty-nine members of the élite of international Couture invited to participate in this show, whose intention is to present, for once, a fusion of ephemeral creativity and eternal beauty to the larger public of museums, art, and fashion. The couturier exhibits fourteen of his creations (red dresses) at the Galleria dell'Accademia.

Valentino is invited to take part in the show "Under Roman Skies," a benefit fashion show organized by RAI. Sharon Stone appears as the designer's special model.

October—the Accademia Valentino hosts a show entitled "Homage to Balthus," which brings together the artist's paintings and graphic works.

1997

Spring–Summer Couture: a collection whose theme is lightness, featuring astonishingly light dresses (some weighing only an ounce!) in chiffon, trimmed with lace, openwork, embroidery, webs lighter than foam. Short is obligatory; the most frequently used colors are gray, lilac, lavender, jade, saffron, and all the tints of spices. Flowers are everywhere, on cashmere suits embroidered with vine shoots, and with slits veiled in tulle, and on short kimono-coats of *Voyage en Orient* inspiration. "Valentino declares his love for women who are light as butterflies, clothing them in an ounce of bold elegance: showing indecent behavior of unspeakable refinement," Paola Pisa comments in the *Messaggero.* "A peak moment with Valentino. The master of elegance has provided one of his most beautiful efforts. In perfect form—even in his stylistic profile—the Italian designer has beaten everyone on the path that guides fashion'97: an unrestrained desire for tenderness," writes the *Washington Post.*

"Botticellian Valentino" is Janie Samet's headline in *Le Figaro.* And she goes on: "Christian Lacroix, sitting among the rows of guests, remained like the rest of us: speechless! The world must not be so ugly if it can inspire such beauty."

Spring–Summer Boutique: the collection exalts luxury and sensuality. "Modern women give more time to love and passion", explains Valentino, "and I have created clothes that harmonize with this new wave of desire." On the stage are trousers of severe cut worn with lace shirts, jumpsuits with strategic transparent insets, plunging necklines that reach the navel, chiffon dresses with fringe that undulates against the legs or with asymmetrical hems. "All the elements blend in this collection, devoted to a woman who is constantly caught up in the game of seduction but always with chic and glamour," Laura Asnaghi writes in the *Repubblica.*

March—the show "Still-Life. The Genius of Evaristo Baschenis" opens at the Accademia Valentino.

May—inaugurates his first Russian boutique, in Moscow.

Fall–Winter Couture: stuns Paris with a collection created for the woman of the third millennium. "Valentino looks to the future. He considers Haute Couture a laboratory in which to experiment with new ideas, and he has designed seventy incomparable outfits that make a clean sweep of the canons of the Haute Couture of the costume museum. In this collection jewels look like pieces of twisted metal, as if melted in the fire of an atomic explosion; the embroidery doesn't have a well-defined pattern but creates weird geometric forms. His women wear suits with chinchilla-edged miniskirts, bird-feather cloaks, sable-trimmed boots.The effect is extremely aggressive," Laura Asnaghi reports in the *Repubblica.*

Fall–Winter Boutique: the collection is devoted to women who are decisive, and perhaps aggressive, yet always sexy, women who do not submit to elegance but dominate it. The collection includes a lot of short skirts and tweed mini-suits with fur collars,

always worn with high boots, in every color and style, in combination with stockings that pick up the pattern. Black abounds; there are tight pants, and sweaters reduced to minimalist elements.

"There are no transparencies, no allusions: here the sensuality is more explicit," declares Valentino.

"Yesterday Valentino succeeded in his intention: he presented a glittering, dynamic show, 25 minutes in all, of clothes that were both sexy and brilliant, thanks to the sparkle of sequins, the embroidery, and the lightness.

There is no need for spectacle when the clothes have something to say," Laura Dubini observes in the *Corriere della Sera.*

September—it is announced that a letter of intent has been signed regarding the acquisition of Valentino and Giancarlo Giammetti's company by HPI, a holding company of industrial shares created from the remains of Gemina, the big financial group whose purpose is to bring together the most important exponents of "made in Italy."

1998

January—makes the sale of his label to HDP (formerly HPI) official.

Making the announcement at a press conference in Milan, the designer, who will thus insure the continuation of his house, cannot contain tears of emotion. And so the name Valentino is listed on the stock exchange.

Spring–Summer Couture 1998: the collection that is shown at the new site, on the Place Vendôme, is the result of the designer's sudden, newfound love for Russia, for St. Petersburg and summer dachas. This surprising development is evident everywhere, in the designs and in the embroidery that embellishes the dresses, with their clean, light lines, in the pink and blue double-cashmere coats, in simple dresses of white doeskin with bead and crystal insets.

In the pages of the *Repubblica*, Laura Asnaghi describes the show as follows: "The guests enter the eighteenth-century palace of the Place Vendôme through an aisle formed by the crowd, to see the most eagerly anticipated show, that of Valentino. Then comes the triumph, and a finale that evokes thunderous applause from the fans and cries of 'Bravo!' Valentino is radiant as he moves through the audience. The clothes inspired by Russia and its dachas are a fairyland of crystal geometries, true masterpieces of the art of Couture. To produce this embroidery which pictures arabesques of ice, winter frosts, and floral fantasies requires

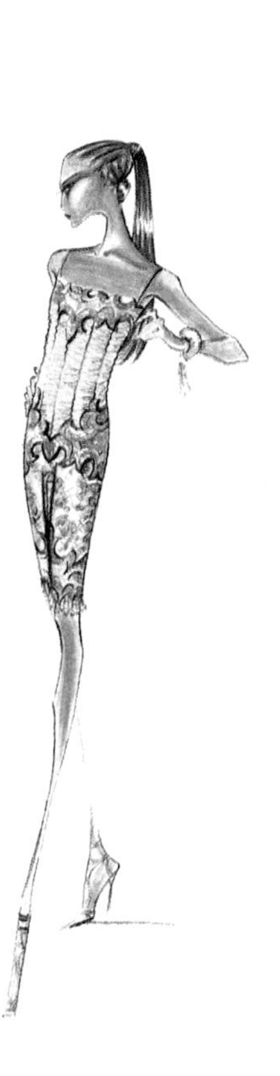

expert hands and countless hours of work."

"Everything is ultra-Valentino, in the femininity of the fox worn over the shoulder under a bouquet of silk flowers, the embroidered taffeta slipper, the evening bag in the form of a shell. And, oddly, this return to the solid values of salon elegance does not seem at all dated. Far from spectacular effects, the woman simply yields to the joy of an exceptional and complete elegance," Janie Samet comments in *Le Figaro*.

The show is also the occasion of the inauguration of the firm's new headquarters in the Place Vendôme, which hosts a sumptuous reception for the event.

Sptring—Summer Boutique 1998: At the Carrousel du Louvre Valentino presents a collection inspired by the American West, with shirts in saloon-style eyelet embroidery studded with rhinestones, miniskirts with bead or jade fringe, skirts of white leather, and of beige, pink, and blue buckskin or reindeer skin. The footwear also follows the cowboy look: white calfskin, snakeskin, and crocodile in vertiginously high boots and sandals.

"Valentino has presented the simplest and at the same time the most luxurious collection of the week," Janie Samet decrees in *Le Figaro*. "On the runway appear millionaire Calamity Janes dressed by a fashion house. Valentino puts on a Western party that is the height of Chic," Paola Pisa writes in the *Messaggero.*

"Valentino's woman is in love with cowboy style. The image of this woman overwhelmed by an uncontrollable passion for everything that recalls Western culture is very seductive," Laura Asnaghi confirms in the *Repubblica.*

At the annual ceremony for the Oscars, in Los Angeles, James Cameron, the director of *Titanic,* which wins eleven Oscars, wears a smoking jacket made by Valentino.

Fall–Winter Boutique—modernity is in the contrasts. Baggy jackets with squared, almost sailor-style necks and chiffon and lace skirts, plus embroidery with kilim-inspired prints, cashmere with beads, studs on tweed. Buttons are replaced by diamond-studded pins.

"Valentino fought back Sunday with an exquisite show, carefully crafted and superbly embellished, to restore faith in High Fashion, " Suzy Menkes writes in the *International Herald Tribune.*

"An homage to luxury, but totally reinvented, suited for a woman who loves refined, discreet elegance," Laura Asnaghi comments in the *Repubblica.*

Page 67

1. Boutique. Fall–Winter 1987–88. Red satin evening gown. Photo Steven Meisel/Archivio Valentino. **2.** Couture. Fall–Winter 1988–89. Red chiffon evening gown with overlapping pleated flounces. Photo Archivio Valentino. **3.** Couture. Fall–Winter 1984–85. Red crêpe evening dress with long V-neckline in back and diamond clasps. Photo J. Noël L'Harmeroult/*Amica.* **4.** Couture. Fall–Winter 1967–68. Red wool brocade suit with tortoise-shell buttons and snakeskin belt with gold V-shaped buckle, fur hat. Photo Archivio Valentino. **5.** Couture. Fall–Winter 1989–90. Black velvet evening dress with red satin cape. Photo Sante D'Orazio/Courtesy *Vogue* © 1989 Les Publications Condé Nast S.A. **6.** Boutique. Fall–Winter 1983–84. Roomy cartwheel mantle in red wool. Photo Fabrizio Ferri/*Donna.* **7.** Couture. Fall–Winter 1987–88. Red wool redingote with high border of brown sable. Photo Arthur Elgort. **8.** Couture. Spring–Summer 1988. Red crêpe and chiffon evening dress, with interlaced, knotted drapery. Photo David Bailey/Archivio Valentino. **9.** Boutique. Fall–Winter 1989–90. Red double wool redingote. Photo Eddy Kohli/*Marie-Claire* © Mondadori Press.

Page 93

1. Couture. Fall–Winter 1963–64. Suit in double wool with dropped sleeves and showy buttons. **2.** Couture. Fall–Winter 1966–67. Space-age look short tunic in white double wool with long tight trousers and little helmet to match. **3.** Couture. Fall–Winter 1962–63. Empire line. Elegant flared overcoat in black wool with high waist, and two buttons and a flat bow at the stand-away collar band; jaguar fur hat. **4.** Couture. Fall–Winter 1962–63. Navy blue and mustard dress and overcoat in double wool with contrasting color inserts; crocodile hat. **5.** Couture. Fall–Winter 1966–67. Geometric-line suit in op art fabric. Photo Regi Relang/Courtesy Verlag Hans Schöner © *30 Jahre Mode Italien.* **6.** Couture. Fall–Winter 1965–66. Black-and-white printed silk minidress with pleated culottes and blouse; wool overcoat with the same print. **7.** Couture. Fall–Winter 1970–71. Dress with short jacket with colored sequins inspired by patchwork quilts. Photo Chris von Wangenheim/Archivio Valentino. **8.** Couture. Fall–Winter 1959–60. Gray redingote with straight skirt, collar and cuffs in brown velvet and otterskin hat. **9.** Couture. Spring–Summer 1970. Maxicoat with fine vertical tucked ribbing and miniskirt. Photo Regi Relang/Courtesy Verlag Hans Schöner © *30 Jahre Mode Italien.* **10.** Couture. Fall–Winter 1965–66. Double-breasted empire-line coat in black-and-white houndstooth pattern. Photo Archivio Valentino. **11.** Couture. Fall–Winter 1962–63. Red wool coat with cockades as buttons. **12.** Couture. Spring–Summer 1969. Beige cloak and vest, white jumpsuit with large patch pockets and gold metal trimming. Photo Archivio Valentino. **13.** Couture. Fall–Winter 1965–66. Classical gray suit with wrap skirt; mink hat. **14.** Couture. Fall–Winter 1970–71. Hooded beige and brown lynx-trimmed suit. Photo Regi Relang/Courtesy Verlag Hans Schöner © *30 Jahre Mode Italien.* **15.** Couture. Fall–Winter 1963–64. Black-and-white suit in ponyskin with fur trim. Photo Archivio Valentino.

Page 94

1. Couture. Fall–Winter 1965–66. Empire-line redingote in raised brocade with small half-belt. **2.** Couture. Fall–Winter 1960–61. Gold lace and brocade amphora-shaped cocktail dress. **3.** Couture. Fall–Winter 1962–63. Black satin evening gown with large bow at the waist and short bolero in gold lace. **4.** Couture. Fall–Winter 1963–64. Heavy pink satin evening gown with short jacket edged in organdy petals. Photo Leombruno Bodi/Archivio Valentino. **5.** Couture. Fall–Winter 1963–64. Empireline evening gown in heavy pink satin with roomy sleeves. **6.** Couture. Spring–Summer 1968. White collection. Gold lamé evening dress relief embroidered in small flower motif; skirt and scarf in silk chiffon; chainlink and wood belt. **7.** Couture. Fall–Winter 1974–75. Folksy palazzo pajama with long-fringed poncho; gold chain and coral belt. Photo Giampaolo Barbieri. **8.** Couture. Fall–Winter 1963–64. Palazzo pajama in white brocade fabric with belt and bow. **9.** Couture. Spring–Summer 1964. Little white organdy jacket with flounced edging over plain black tube dress. Photo Regi Relang/Courtesy Verlag Hans Schöner © *30 Jahre Mode Italien.* **10.** Couture. Spring–Summer 1967. Veruschka. Palazzo pajama in cotton satin with large panthers printed in black on a green ground. Photo Franco Rubartelli. **11.** Couture. Fall–Winter 1968–69. White silk evening gown. **12.** Couture. Fall–Winter 1961–62. Two-piece evening dress with jet-and gemstone-trimmed tunic. **13.** Couture. Fall–Winter 1968–69. Polka-dot palazzo pajama in white organdy with giant daisy edging. Photo David Bailey/Courtesy *Vogue* © 1968 Edizioni Condé Nast S.p.A. **14.** Couture. Spring–Summer 1959. Evening dress with petticoated white satin skirt and black chiffon blouse, decorated with two large white roses. Photo Archivio Valentino. **15.** Couture. Fall–Winter 1963–64. Low-waisted pink satin cocktail dress with amphora-shaped skirt; ruched neckline with tulle rose. Photo Archivio Valentino. **16.** Couture. Fall–Winter 1959–60. White satin cocktail dress printed with floral motifs inspired by bougainvillea. Photo Archivio Valentino.

Page 134

1. Boutique. Fall–Winter 1989–90. Black velvet evening dress with white draping. Photo Walter Chin/Archivio Valentino. **2.** Couture. Fall–Winter 1965–66. Blue-and-white coat with op art motifs. Photo Archivio Valentino. **3.** Couture. Spring–Summer 1966. Dress with black-and-white op art motif. Photo Archivio Valentino. **4.** Couture. Fall–Winter 1989–90. Detail of jacket embroidered with decorative motif inspired by Hoffmann. Photo Janos Grapow/Archivio Valentino. **5.** Couture. Fall–Winter 1989–90. Crocodile, white lizard, and python skin purse with motifs inspired by Hoffmann. Photo Archivio Valentino. **6.** Couture. Spring–Summer 1969. Trouser suit with print inspired by Beardsley. Photo François Leroy-Beaulieu/Archivio Valentino. **7.** Couture. Spring–Summer 1969. Dress with geometrical appliqué motif. Photo David Bailey/Archivio Valentino. **8.** Couture. Spring–Summer 1970. Blouse in op art fabric with "Valentino" written in various sizes. Photo Archivio Valentino. **9.** Couture. Spring–Summer 1987. Evening gown with strongly contrasted black-and-white chevron motif. Photo David Bailey/Archivio Valentino. **10.** Couture. Fall–Winter 1965–66. White chamois boots with black pom-poms. Photo Archivio Valentino. **11.** Couture. Fall–Winter 1967–68. Checked and striped suit with striking black-and-white graphic motifs. Photo Archivio Valentino. **12.** Couture. Fall–Winter 1966–67. Dress and overcoat with geometric motifs inspired by Vasarely's paintings. Photo Archivio Valentino. **13.** Couture. Spring–Summer 1966. Two black-and-white sequin suits and "box" hats. Photo Henry Clarke/Courtesy *Vogue* © 1966 Condé Nast Publications Inc.

Page 146

1. Couture. Spring–Summer 1987. Ribbons laced through loops in printed silk dresses. Photo Archivio Valentino. **2.** Couture. Spring–Summer 1983. Evening gown with large bow at back. Photo Marco Glaviano/Archivio Valentino. **3.** Couture. Spring–Summer 1983. Detail of wide-brimmed hat with large bow at the front. Photo Arthur Elgort/Archivio Valentino. **4.** Couture. Fall–Winter 1987–88. Red evening dress with asymmetrical hem and large black bow. Photo David Bailey/Archivio Valentino. **5.** Boutique. Fall–Winter 1987–88. Black velvet dress featuring a white ribbon looped through the sleeve. Photo Archivio Valentino. **6.** Couture. Fall–Winter 1967–68. Sergio Valente's hairstyle with bows for Valentino. Photo Archivio Valentino. **7.** Couture. Spring–Summer 1989. Evening gown with white collar and black bows. Photo David Bailey/Archivio Valentino. **8.** Couture. Fall–Winter 1987–88. Detail of overlapped neckline with looped bow. Photo Gianni Giansanti/Sygma/Grazia Neri. **9.** Boutique. Fall–Winter 1982–83. Black velvet evening dress with large bow and white quilted peplum. Photo Rico Puhlmann/Archivio Valentino.

Page 152

Accessories. **1.** Jewelry. Fall–Winter 1984–85. Large bow cuff bracelet. Photo Oliviero Toscani/Archivio Valentino. **2.** Couture. Fall–Winter 1985–86. Eighteenth-century style rhinestone jewlery. Photo Terence Donovan/Archivio Valentino. **3.** Couture. Fall–Winter 1985–86. Ornament in the shape of bows of diminishing sizes. Photo Archivio Valentino. **4.** Couture. Fall–Winter 1982–83. Black evening dress with asymmetrical neckline and white sash with large bow at the shoulder. Photo Barry McKinley/Archivio Valentino. **5.** Boutique. Fall–Winter 1985–86. Draped red dress with black bow clasp. Photo Terence Donovan/Archivio Valentino. **6.** Boutique. Spring–Summer 1984. Detail of bow bracelet. Photo Helmut Newton/Archivio Valentino. **7.** Couture. Fall–Winter 1984–85. Detail of white evening dress with bared back, closed by a bow. Photo Arthur Elgort/Courtesy *Vogue* © 1985 Les Publications Condé Nast S.A. **8.** Couture. Spring–Summer 1985. Detail of draped red evening gown and black how clasps. Photo John Swannell/Archivio Valentino. **9.** Boutique. Spring–Summer 1985. Jeweled bow on back of evening gown. Photo Irving Penn/Courtesy *Vogue* © 1985 Condé Nast Publications Inc. **10.** Couture. Spring–Summer 1984. Detail of bowshaped jewelry. Photo Helmut Newton/Archivio Valentino.

Page 162

1. Couture. Spring–Summer 1969. Little double-polka-dot dress and transparent polka-dot tights. Photo Archivio Valentino. **2.** Couture. Spring–Summer 1971. Maxi polka-dot chemisier open in front and cinched by a belt with oriental-style buckle over short shorts with fishnet tights. Photo Bob Krieger. **3.** Couture. Spring–Summer 1983. Silk tunic with large polka-dot motif; white cuffs and skirt; broad-brimmed hat with large bow. Photo Avi Meroz. **4.** Couture. Spring–Summer 1983. Chinese-style tunics over trousers with small polkadot motif in negative and positive. Photo Yokosuka/Archivio Valentino. **5.** Les Enfants. Fall–Winter 1984–85. Polka-dot dress with large bow and white collar. Photo Danilo Frontini/Archivio Valentino. **6.** Boutique. Spring–Summer 1984. Suit with long polka-dot silk jacket, tight skirt, and "sailor" style beret. Photo Helmut Newton/Archivio Valentino. **7.** Couture. Spring–Summer 1983. Polka-dot silk evening gown with drapery and knotted bows. Photo Giampaolo Barbieri. **8.** Couture. Spring–Summer 1987. Austere "school girl" evening dress with large white collar. Photo Cristina Ghergo/Archivio Valentino. **9.** Couture. Spring–Summer 1988. Black suit with black-and-white polka-dot scarf. Photo David Bailey/Archivio Valentino.

Page 283

1. Couture. Fall–Winter 1985–86. Evening dress with plunging neckline and an embroidered skirt. Photo Terence Donovan. **2.** Couture. Fall–Winter 1986–87. Dress in large floral print fabric and matching wrap. Photo Oliviero Toscani. **3.** Couture. Fall–Winter 1982–83. Evening gown featuring a velvet bodice trimmed with red and purple, scalloped taffeta flounces and a long, side-slit, red crêpe skirt. Photo Barry McKinley. **4.** Couture. Fall–Winter 1986–87. Ball gown with severe line and gold fur hat and belt. Photo Terence Donovan/*L'Officiel*. **5.** Couture. Fall–Winter 1990–91. Brown draped dress. Photo David Bailey/Archivio Valentino. **6.** Couture. Fall–Winter 1989–90. Polka-dot evening dress. Photo Walter Chin. **7.** Couture. Spring–Summer 1988. Crinoline dress with, wide horizontal black, white, and pink bands. Photo David Bailey. **8.** Couture. Fall–Winter 1983–84. Black sequined evening dress with "galaxy" motif embroidered over one shoulder and long-fringed sleeves. Photo Barry McKinley. **9.** Couture. Fall–Winter 1990–91. Jet-beaded evening dress with bow at the waist. Photo David Bailey.

Page 286

1. Couture. Spring–Summer 1987. Balck evening dress with short torero-style bolero embroidered with seedbeads. Photo Alex Chatelain/Archivio Valentino. **2.** Couture. Fall–Winter 1986–87. Jewellike bodice all in openwork embroidery with sable trim and brown velvet skirt. Photo François Lamy/Courtesy *Harper's Bazaar Italia*. **3.** Boutique. Fall–Winter 1988–89. Elegant evening gown with Louis XVI-style embroidered bodice, with black and silver sequins, over a midnight blue taffeta and lace skirt. **4.** Couture. Fall–Winter 1988–89. Satin evening dress with sable-trimmed jacket, embroidered with baroque-inspired motifs. Photo David Bailey. **5.** Couture. Fall–Winter 1988–89. Blue evening dress with draped bodice, corset belt with exquisite embroidery; satin skirt and flowing wrap. Photo David Bailey. **6.** Boutique. Fall–Winter 1986–87. Black evening dress with cuffs and sash in gold. Photo David Bailey. **7.** Couture. Fall–Winter 1989–90. Satin evening gown with embroidery and appliqué flowers on off-the-shoulder fitted sleeves; interlaced ribbons at the necklirel accent the bodice. Photo Matthew Rolston. **8.** Boutique. Spring–Summer 1990. Silk crêpe evening gown with exquisite insets of embroidered flowers with silver leaves. Photo Eamonn J. McCabe/*Marie-Claire* © Mondadori Press. **9.** Boutique. Fall–Winter 1987–88. Pink satin evening dress with fitted bodice and double peplum.